THE ART OF
Decoration

*God Bless you,
Dahlia Zárate-Muniz
Matthew 19:26*

THE ART OF *Decoration*
A Sacred Tribute to God

Dahlia Zárate-Muñiz
& Maria Arias-Lucio

Tate Publishing & *Enterprises*

The Art of Decoration
Copyright © 2011 by Dahlia Zárate-Muñiz & Maria Arias-Lucio. All rights reserved.

No part of this publication may be reproduced, stored in a retrieval system or transmitted in any way by any means, electronic, mechanical, photocopy, recording or otherwise without the prior permission of the author except as provided by USA copyright law.

Scripture quotations marked (NIV) are taken from the Holy Bible, New International Version®, NIV®. Copyright © 1973, 1978, 1984 by Biblica, Inc.™ Used by permission of Zondervan. All rights reserved worldwide. www.zondervan.com

The opinions expressed by the author are not necessarily those of Tate Publishing, LLC.

Published by Tate Publishing & Enterprises, LLC
127 E. Trade Center Terrace | Mustang, Oklahoma 73064 USA
1.888.361.9473 | www.tatepublishing.com

Tate Publishing is committed to excellence in the publishing industry. The company reflects the philosophy established by the founders, based on Psalm 68:11,
"The Lord gave the word and great was the company of those who published it."

Book design copyright © 2011 by Tate Publishing, LLC. All rights reserved.
Cover décor inspired by God Al Mighty to Dahlia Zárate-Muñiz
Graphic design by Amber Gulilat
Interior design by Christina Hicks

Published in the United States of America

ISBN: 978-1-61777-312-9
1. Religion / Christian Life / Stewardship & Giving
2. Religion / Christian Ministry / General
11.04.28

DEDICATION

To give praise, honor, and glory to God, this book is dedicated to my Holy Father and to future generations.

This book is God inspired and could not have been written without him. I am humbled and very honored that my Holy Father chose me to write this book.

ACKNOWLEDGEMENTS:
Dahlia Zárate-Muñiz

With special thanks:

First and foremost, I want to thank my Almighty God. Thank You, my Holy Father, for Your love, mercy and grace. Thank You for Your son Jesus Christ of Nazareth. Thank You for allowing me to share with the world about Your miracles and wonders and the immense love You have for all of us sinners. Thank You for my life. Thank You for your abundant blessings.

To my beloved husband Andy Muñiz, for the love and support given me during the writing of this book. Thank you for your prayers, for always providing for me and for your good cooking. You're simply the best!

To my blood sister Rosalinda Hernández Zárate, thank you for being my sister, for your love, your support, and faithful prayers.

To my beautiful niece whom I love as a daughter, Sonya Herrera Hernández, thank you for your love, for being you, and most of all for your prayers when I needed them the most.

To my cousin Adalberto (Cookie) Hernández, thank you for your love, your life-saving and faithful prayers.

To Apostle Dr. Genovevo and Pastora Juanita Izaguirre, thank you for your love, your spiritual guidance, and faithful prayers. Thank you for your obedience to our Almighty God and the love you have for our Lord.

To my sister in Christ Sylvia Vera, thank you for your prayers, your wisdom, and your support . I will treasure your valuable contributions forever.

To the Intercessors from *Iglesia Misión Divina Centrál*, thank you for your prayers on this project that my Holy Father instructed me to do.

To my sister in Christ Julia Fuentes, thank you for your love, your obedience to our Lord and for your prayers.

To all of my family and friends that have prayed for me at one time or another throughout my lifetime. God Bless you.

To Maria de la Luz Arias-Lucio, last but not least; my partner, my sister in Christ whom I love as a daughter. Thank you for being you, for being obedient to our Lord and for loving him. Because of you, many years ago when I needed it the most; you showed me that besides my family, there are caring people in this world after all. I wanted that same love you had for our Lord, I asked him and he answered my prayers.

I pray that God give you all wisdom, peace, love, endurance, strength, and good health to finish the race triumphantly. May he give you all eternal life. I love you all. *Amen!*

ACKNOWLEDGEMENTS:
Maria Arias-Lucio

With special thanks:

I would like to thank my Holy Father for having chosen me to relay his will to Sister Dahlia. I also thank him for my life and all the blessings he has given me and my family.

> Give thanks to the Lord, for he is good. His love endures forever.
>
> Psalm 136:1

Parents

I like to thank my parents Juan Arias Bautista and Constanza Mendoza Arias for planting a beautiful seed in my heart as a child to believe in God's promise.

> Train a child in the way he should go, and when he is old he will not turn from it.
>
> Proverbs 22:6

Thank you for always being there for me and keeping me in your prayers. I love you.

For my sister Martha Aracely Arias, I am really grateful to have a caring and loving sister like you.

Thank you for your prayers and support, may God bless you always.

Family

To my husband and my three unique and beautiful children Sabina del Carmen Lucio, Martha Constanza Lucio and Felipe (Little Prophet) Rumaldo Lucio for their patience, love, and understanding (in their own little way). Sabina, thank you for your prayers and love you have for Jesus in your heart for you are really special to me and I believe God will guide and will help you make a difference in this world one day. I love you all!

Spiritual Family

For all my brothers and sisters in Christ who always had a smile for me and were always there to encourage me through my experience and who always believed and kept their faith that God in his great mercy would work with me and bring me back to his flock. I would specially like to recognize Sister Irene Gonzalez, Sister Rosita Karr, Sister Andreita Garcia, Sister Panchita Garcia, Sister Juanita Mercado, and Sister Serene Rodriguez.

Brother Francisco (Paco) Gonzalez, thank you for your advice and teachings that I received from you as a teacher. They have immensely helped and have been a huge blessing in my life. Equally the beautiful singing ministry that God gave you and your family. May God continue to strengthen you all and continue using you with more potency and power for God's glory and honor. Thank you for always being there for me and my family.

I want to specially thank Sister Julia Fuentes: in good times and in bad times you have always been with my family at all hours to pray for us and to give us God's word no matter the situation. You are always there for God's calling and always willing to help without fail. Besides being a member of a church and having been obedient to God, you founded a beautiful mission in Matamoros, Tamaulipas, Mexico named *Misión Cristiana Cristo Vive* in the midst of such great oppression. May God bless you always and give you strength so that you may continue to and accomplish your heart's desire to build another mission in the same city.

I like to take this opportunity to acknowledge Mrs. Dahlia Zárate-Muñiz, a woman I have learned to love, respect, and trust as a mom. When I first met Ms. Dahlia, as I used to call her in our old work place, it never crossed my mind I was going to hold a permanent friendship with her, but God knew his plan. Our friendship grew and no matter how near or far I was, we always kept in touch. When God brought me back from Florida, I noticed God was working with Ms. Dahlia unto a spiritual level where she was to see God's glory in a tremendous way. Ms. Beautiful, as God and I call her now (because she is beautiful in God's hands!), has been a great blessing in my life, and I am awed as to how God works in our lives. Ms. Beautiful testified she asked God for the same love I had for him, and God gave her that love, saved her, and blessed her with a unique ministry. Sister Dahlia made a special prayer to God to return all those who had one day worked with God and worshiped him to come back to the flock again, and God heard her. Unknowingly she prayed for me and my cousins as well, and Easter of 2009 we worked on the rock after many years of not teaming up to work for God and leading then to my awakening. Thank you, Ms. Beautiful, for always being there, for your advice, your patience, understanding, your prayers, and for just being you. You will always have a special place in my heart.

I like to thank your husband our beloved friend and brother-in-Christ Andy Muñiz for your prayers and always being there, too.

For all, I pray and ask Jesus to cover you and your families with his holy blood; to always guide and protect you. To send his angels around you, guide and bless you all in a very special way. I ask in Jesus name, amen!

TABLE OF CONTENTS

Preface	15
Introduction	17
Prologue	19
Department's Role	25
Planning	29
Meetings	31
Reports	33
Samples	35
Funds	43
Accomplishments	45
Materials Used	47
Purchasing Supplies	49
Decorating The Temple	51
Recognize Department's Potential And Importance	55
Decorations In The Temple	59

Supernatural Connection/ Communication	67
Pictures	73
Spiritual Decorations	85
Testimonies	93
About The Authors	139
Mision Divina's Ornamentation Department Logo	147
Symbolism Colors	153
Symbolism Numbers	159
Closing	163
Church Name And Address	165
Contact The Authors	167
Resources	169

PREFACE

I adore God for knowing Sister Dahlia Muñiz who arrived at *Iglesia Misión Divina Centrál*, Brownsville, Texas, USA, of which I am the founding pastor. Our sister came to our church in 2007 and has been an official member since 2009.

God put in my heart that she direct the Ornamentation Department for the church because of the love that she has for our Lord, and the experience obtained in her past, working with different governmental agencies at a local, state, and federal level.

Dahlia has shown a beautiful spiritual growth; I believe she is an honorable person and loves God with all of her heart. Our sister is very knowledgeable and is excellent in coordinating and organizing. She has been a huge blessing in the church. The whole church is happy with the work and the manner in which she decorates the church.

I believe this book that our Lord has put in her heart will be a huge blessing not only to this church but to the church in general. I bless the work of her hands and I recommend that all who love God's house and feel it in their heart to follow the footsteps of this beautiful ministry.

Yours in Jesus,
Apostle Dr. Genovevo Izaguirre
Brownsville, Texas, USA

INTRODUCTION

On February 15, 2010, my sister in Christ Mary Lucio called me, all excited. She told me to get something to write with; she had some information I needed to write down. After she gave me all the information, she said, "You have in front of you the title and chapters of a book." God had given her the title and chapters of a book that he wanted us to write. I love Mary and have known her for many years. She is a very intelligent woman with many gifts and strengths. However, decorating is not her forte. Based on the information she gave me I knew instantly that it was Divine Wisdom. God works in mysterious ways, so believe me, this book was God inspired.

I am humbled and honored that my Holy Father chose me to write this book; to my knowledge, an unchartered territory. I am not an author; never in my wildest dreams did I ever think that I would write a book. But with God, all things are possible!

Mary and I pray that this book will be an enormous blessing. We pray that it will help educate the reader on how to hear God's voice and be obedient regarding the decorations for his house of worship. Mary and I pray that this book will enlighten the reader about the impact decorations have, not only on the earthly realm, but in the spiritual realm as well.

In addition, this book is based on my personal experiences as the director of the Ornamentation Department. I will share several testimonies about the miracles and wonders that transpired as God led me to *Iglesia Misión Divina Centrál*, and the miracles and wonders that occurred during my tenure. My God is a great and marvelous God.

PROLOGUE

At a very young age, I was motivated to look at the symbolism of events, objects, and colors in my life. This word "symbolism" always came to mind, and now more than ever.

I never knew that God wanted to establish a personal relationship with us. However, since I began decorating the temple, I have learned that God is constantly talking to us. When we establish a personal relationship with him, we will learn to discern when he speaks to us. God speaks to us through scriptures as well as apart from the Bible. He speaks through visions, prophets, angels, prompting (to urge into action), dreams, intuition, and thoughts. My Holy Father also speaks through numbers, colors, decorations, heavenly signs, people, music, bill boards, audible voice, and many other ways.

I acknowledge the Bible warns us about false christs and prophets:

> For false Christs and false prophets will appear and perform signs and miracles to deceive the elect…
>
> Mark 13: 22

> Watch out for false prophets....By their fruit you will recognize them....A good tree cannot bear bad fruit, and a bad tree cannot bear good fruit.
>
> Matthew 7:15-18

Good fruit is recognized by the following:

> But the fruit of the Spirit is love, joy, peace, patience, kindness, goodness faithfulness, gentleness and self-control.
>
> Galations 5:22-24

However, the Bible also states that God speaks to us in many ways:

> All scripture is God breathed and is useful for teaching, rebuking, correcting and training in righteousness, so that the man of God may be thoroughly equipped for every good work.
>
> 2 Timothy 3:16-17

> He said, listen to my words: 'When a prophet of the Lord is among you, I reveal myself to him in visions, I speak to him in dreams. But this is not true of my servant Moses, he is faithful in all my house. With him I speak face to face.'
>
> Numbers 12: 6-8

> In the last days, God says, I will pour out my spirit on all people. Your sons and daughters will prophesy, your young men will see

visions, your old men will dream dreams. Even on my servants, both men and women, I will pour out my Spirit in those days, and they will prophesy. I will show wonders in the heaven above and signs on the earth below…

Acts 2:17-19

During the night Paul had a vision…

Acts 16:9

But God has revealed it to us by his Spirit.

1 Corinthians 2:10

This is what we speak, not in words taught us by human wisdom but in words taught by the Spirit, expressing spiritual truths in spiritual words.

1 Corinthians 2:13

God spoke to our forefathers through the prophets at many times and in various ways.

Hebrews 1:1

God also testified to it by signs, wonders and various miracles…

Hebrews 2:4

He made it known by sending his angel to his servant…

Revelation 1:1

The Lord, the God of the spirits of the prophets, sent his angel to show his servants the things that must soon take place.

> Revelation 22:6

See to it that you do not refuse him who speaks...

> Hebrews 12:25

Then the Lord called Samuel...

> 1 Samuel 3:4

He who has an ear, let him hear what the Spirit says to the churches.

> Revelation 3:22

So whatever I say is just what the Father has told me to say.

> John 12:50

It is the Father living in me, who is doing his work.

> John 14:10

These words you hear are not my own; they belong to the Father...

> John 14:24

The Holy Spirit, whom the Father will send in my name, will teach you all things and will remind you...

> John 14:26

So that we won't easily be deceived, it is very important we establish a personal relationship with God. It is crucial that one seeks God, prays, fasts, and reads the Bible.

DEPARTMENT'S ROLE

I have learned that our Lord speaks and manifests through the decorations. Consequently, the Department's role is not only to beautify the Lord's house of worship, but to also ensure his message is conveyed in a visual manner. Prayer, discernment, and communication are vital.

There is protocol and order that needs to be followed, as well as planning. I also need to stress that God is a God of order; the Holy Bible is a testament to that.

> For God is not a God of disorder…
>
> 1 Corinthians 14:33

> But everything should be done in a fitting and orderly way.
>
> 1 Corinthians 14:40

> There is a time for everything, and a season for every activity under heaven: a time to be born and a time to die; a time to plant and a time to uproot; a time to kill and a time to heal…
>
> Ecclesiastes 3:1-8

Therefore, as a servant of God, one needs to do his will in an orderly manner.

It is a privilege and an honor to beautify the Lord's house of worship. One's focus should be on our Lord, to please him, be loyal, obedient and to honor him. One must always remember that it is for him and him alone that one decorates for. No one else!

In order that one ensures one is doing God's will, one will need to fast, pray, and ask him for his guidance. Pray! Pray! Pray! Ask him for discernment, he will give you discernment.

> Pray that the Lord your God will tell us where we should go and what we should do."
>
> Jeremiah 42:3

You might ask, how does one discern what God wants? One way is, God will put an idea into your mind, but it is up to us whether we act upon it or not. God is always talking to us. Ask him for confirmation, so be alert and look at your surroundings.

> The skies proclaim the work of his hands. Day after day they pour forth speech; night after night they display knowledge. There is no speech or language where their voice is not heard. Their voice goes out into all the earth."
>
> Psalm 19:1-4

He will answer through a person, music, a billboard, animal, color, number, picture, and many other ways. Listen to your inner voice, which many call your gut feeling.

I cannot stress the importance of communication. I believe this is very important in every situation. There is protocol that needs to be followed; consequently, communication is essential. Communication should be with the pastor and other departments, as well as within the Ornamentation Department. Without communication, one might and will encounter misunderstandings, and hurt feelings. Do not be afraid to speak up and voice your suggestions and/or recommendations; one should be receptive to these. Ensure that all is understood; therefore, do not be afraid to ask questions if you do not understand. One should also be considerate with one another. Some people are visual and some are slower than others to grasp what one is trying to convey.

Honor God by respecting everyone, including those in positions with authority. This applies to all. God only knows why he wants that individual in that position. One may encounter animosity between members of the congregation and other individuals with authority. One may also be criticized by the decision one makes. However, always keep in mind that the individuals are ignorant of many things and might not understand the decisions one makes. I need to clarify that thanks to my Lord, I have not encountered animosity with the leaders in our church, nor with any members of the congregation. But remember we have an enemy (Satan) that is always looking for ways to create animosity, dissension, and more. He never sleeps! Whatever you do, do not compromise God's will!

PLANNING

To help plan, implement, and execute the functions of the department, the following are a few steps that you might want to take into consideration. I believe these will help in the preparation and organization of the department. I have also included a sample monthly expenditure report, an agenda, a schedule, a plan, a certificate of appreciation and a thank you letter. These are very simple, yet effective, so for the sake of time and for documentation purposes, I believe these will suffice. On the other hand, you can customize to fit your needs.

First, choose the holidays and events the Ornamentation Department will want to undertake. These might be Easter, Christmas, Thanksgiving, the four seasons of the year (that is, winter, spring, summer, and autumn seasons), Holy Supper, church anniversary, conferences, etc.

Decide what the decorations will cover, such as the altar, the whole temple, the main entrance, and so on. Be specific on the dates the temple will be decorated. For example: Christmas–beginning December 1 through December 31, and so forth.

Determine whether minimal decorations will be done at the main entrance for certain holidays such as Valentine's Day, Mother's Day, Father's Day, and Independence Day. Specify when and for how long the decorations will be up for these holidays. For example: For one week, the week leading up to the holiday, Valentine's Day—February 8 to February 14.

Of course, for special events you will need to select the appropriate decorations. These special occasions or events such as the Holy Supper, church anniversary, conferences, and so on will need special planning.

Second, type the schedule of the special events, holidays, conferences, etc. you have decided to undertake. Include the actual dates the temple will be decorated and high light the actual holiday on the schedule. This will make it easier when referring to the schedule. Include the names and contact information of all the members in the Ornamentation Department on the schedule.

Third, submit the schedule to your pastor for approval. Be flexible with your schedule, it is not written in stone. Changes might occur during the year and the schedule will need to be modified. Once approved, provide a copy to all of the members in the department.

MEETINGS

As part of the planning process, it is very important to schedule meetings with the Ornamentation Department members to discuss and strategize the decorating ideas for the appropriate holiday/event. Meetings should be held in an orderly manner and scheduled with ample time to discuss decorations for the holiday. One needs to have enough time to purchase the material for the appropriate holiday. Therefore, a written agenda for each meeting is highly recommended. The agenda should include the items that will be discussed. This will assist in keeping order and not deviate from the subject.

Punctuality is very important, given that many of the members are volunteers. One needs to be considerate about their families, jobs, and so forth. So if a meeting is scheduled at a certain hour, one should commence the meeting at that hour. The members of the department should also be made aware that they need to be responsible about attending. One should not have to call each member to remind them about a scheduled meeting. If the meeting is canceled and/or postponed, then it is the director's responsibility to call and inform the members. If a member will not be able to attend, it is the member's responsibility to call and inform the director.

Always begin the meetings with a prayer and ask our Lord for harmony, guidance, discernment, and creativity. Remember, these meetings are to strategize, share ideas, and ensure it is what/how God wants his temple decorated. One should not be offended nor take it personally when their idea is or was not approved. Honor God; do not get upset if things do not go as planned. There is a reason for it, and it is always for the best.

It is important that we put in written form what comes to mind, such as drawings and sketches. As I mentioned before, God puts an idea on our minds; it is up to us whether we act upon it or not. At the meetings, all should share what God has given to each individual. It may be that two or three or all come to the table with the same ideas. This is how one discerns what our Holy Father wants.

REPORTS

As mentioned before, communication is very important. So, on a monthly basis, the Ornamentation Department Director should submit reports to the pastor. Reports such as plans, schedules, meetings, copy of agendas, yearly plans, departmental expenditures, or anything else that the pastor requires.

As a best practice, it is recommended that receipts of all expenditures be kept for each month. Keep copies of the reports and everything else submitted to the pastor. Knowing how the enemy works (he comes to destroy), it is also recommended that an actual paper file is kept for the reports besides the ones in your computer.

SAMPLES

1. Agenda
2. Decoration schedule
3. Expenditure report
4. Decoration Department Plan
5. Thank you letter
6. Certificate of appreciation

(Name of Church)

Ornamentation Department
Meeting Agenda
(Date & Time)

1. Pray

2. Communicate! Communicate! Communicate!

3. Put in written form ideas, i.e. sketch ideas, draw, etc.

4. Major event

5. Funds

6. Business cards—name, phone number, etc.

Let's keep in mind; be obedient to our Holy Father, honor Him in all that we do in our daily lives, walk in righteousness. Amen.

(Name of Church)

Ornamentation Department
Decorations for (Year)

The decorations will encompass special events, holidays, and the winter, spring, summer and autumn seasons. This schedule is tentative and subject to change. Actual holiday is reflected in color.

Both the altar and the entrance will be decorated for the following:

- Spring—Beginning March 1
- Palm Sunday—March 28
- Easter Sunday—March 29-April 4
- Fall/Thanksgiving—September 23-November 30
- Christmas—Beginning December 1-December 31

Minimal decorations will be done at the entrance for only one week. The week leading up to the holiday (unless an extension is requested) for the following:

- Valentine's Day—February 8-February 14
- Mother's Day—May 3-May 9
- Father's Day—June 14-June 20
- Independence Day—June 28-July 4

Appropriate decorations for the following special occasions:

- Holy Supper—As scheduled
- Church Anniversary—November 7
- Revival themes
- Conferences

(Name) – Director
(Phone number)
(Name) – Assistant
(Phone number)

(Name of Church)

Ornamentation Department
Expenditure Report
(Month and Year)

Expenditures for the Decoration Department
Totaled to (enter amount)

Funds Used Were for the Purchase of the Following:

Christmas tablecloths
Christmas table Napkins
Christmas Garlands
Holly
Christmas Picks
Ribbons
Vase
Poinsettias
Floral Accents
Sodas for Concert
Thread
Curtain Rod
Butterflies
Material for Red Panels
Gasoline
Meals

(Name of Church)

Ornamentation Department
(Year) Plan

The Decoration Department's plan for the year (2009) is as follows:

A. Decorations: We will meet about two weeks prior to decorating the church with ideas in written form (e.g., sketches, drawings) to ensure we are all in agreement that it is what our Holy Father wants. This will be for all events, occasions, holidays, and seasons.

B. Anniversary: About three months before the anniversary, the department needs/wants to meet with pastor to strategize and come up with a plan of decoration for this event.

Funds: (Name of individual) will solicit donations from the community. To begin this endeavor the following will be followed:

1. Department will allot ($ enter amount) for gas and food.
2. He /She will submit a plan which will include dates/days, places he/she will contact or plan to contact.
3. He/she will submit receipts for gas and food expenditures.
4. He/she will be provided with a picture ID which reflects his membership in (Church Name).
5. He/she will be provided with Department's business cards, they will reflect (Church Name), address, and website, his /her name, and telephone number.
6. He/she will dress appropriately when requesting donations, after all, he/she is representing our Holy Father.
7. The Department will make a 10% offering of all funds donated to (Church Name). The offering will be applied to (specify such as radio, television show, etc.).
8. The business/individual will be provided with a letter which asks for a donation (the letter can be used for their tax write-off).
9. A thank you letter will be given to the business/individual that gives a donation.

(Name), Director
Ornamentation Department

(Name of Church)

(Date)

Dear Friend,

I would like to take this opportunity to thank you for your generosity. Giving to the purposes of God is also a seed that will reap a harvest.

Knowing we have the support of people like you in our community is certainly a huge blessing.

If I can ever be of any assistance, please do not hesitate to contact me at (phone number) or (e-mail address).

Once again, thank you very much for your contribution.

God Bless you,

(Pastor's name)

(Church address)

(City, State, zip code)

(Website)

FUNDS

God has given us freedom as to how we do things. I chose to stay and worship him and be in his presence. As a result he blessed me tremendously. I started the department with zero funds, and now I always have the funds to purchase the materials needed. However, we also have to do our part in raising funds and not leave it all to God.

There are many ways one can raise funds for the department. The department may organize car washes, solicit donations, have a bake sale and sell cakes, cupcakes, cookies, etc. Sell candies, lunch plates, have a garage sale. One can also search the internet for fundraising ideas and resources.

ACCOMPLISHMENTS

Honor those who volunteered in the department as well as those God wants for you to honor. Fast, pray, and ask God how he wants to recognize those individuals.

Talk to your pastor and let him know that you would like to acknowledge the volunteers during a Sunday service. Depending on your funds, they can be presented with a certificate of appreciation, a plaque, or small gift.

My Holy Father chose this year to honor Pastor Genovevo Izaguirre and *Misión Divina*. My Holy Father instructed me to accomplish this as well. A United States flag was flown over our nation's capitol in honor of Pastor Genovevo and Juanita Izaguirre and *Misión Divina's* twenty-fourth anniversary. He also opened the doors so that I would get an autographed picture of the first American of Mexican descent astronaut in space a week after his return from space, and I obtained a personal thank you video message from Astronaut Jose Hernandez to the pastor and *Iglesia Misión Divina Central*.

Have a year in review by presenting a power point presentation during this special ceremony. The power point presentation should include decorations, as well as all accomplishments by the department for that year. Give a brief to the church regarding what they are about to view. This report may include an introduction, what the department consisted of, accomplishments, funds, expenditures, and testimonies of miracles that occurred throughout the year.

You may view the Ornamentation Department's power point presentation for 2009 at *Misión Divina's* website at www.misiondivina.com.

MATERIALS USED

The materials one uses for the decorations should be new, clean, pure, and nothing from the trash can. My Holy Father's house and altar are sacred. I strongly believe he deserves the best one can afford to bring into his house of worship, after all, he is the one that gives us life, good health, sanity, children, food, the air we breathe. I could go on and on.

I was extremely careful about what I took into the temple. I did not want to offend my Holy Father by bringing in trash, nor did I want to jeopardize *Misión Divina's* ministry. When one brings into the temple something that is not pleasing or is offensive to God, it can have negative repercussions. God can be grieved to the point that his presence will no longer be felt. Ephesians 4:30, "And do not grieve the Holy Spirit of God…"

For example: (to paraphrase) If you recall the Prophet Jonah eaten by a whale? God had instructed Jonah to go to Nineveh and preach, however, Jonah refused and fled on a ship. Jonah was asleep, there was a great storm. The sailors almost lost their lives. The Captain and sailors innocently going about their business were also being punished for something not of their doing.

Another example: (to paraphrase) in the book of Joshua in chapter seven; because of the disloyalty to the Lord, one man stole from the Lord and violated God's covenant. It adversely affected the entire nation, and a curse fell upon them.

On account of one individual going against the Lord, everyone will suffer the consequences. Therefore, it is critical that one is extremely careful of what is brought into the Lord's house.

PURCHASING SUPPLIES

Whatever supplies one purchases for decorations, make sure they are the best you can afford. The highest quality materials and fabrics ought to be used. Always purchase the supplies for each holiday with ample time.

There will be times that you will purchase something automatically without thinking. Before you know it, God will put it in our heart to use it on a decoration or use it as a decoration. This happened to me several times as I shopped for the supplies.

One must also be obedient to God when out shopping for supplies. When he tells you no more, it means no more. Last Christmas I got a bit carried away. There were many beautiful things and they were also marked down. I remember picking up a decoration and he said, "No more." Let me tell you, I did not hesitate one bit. I set that little jewel down real quick. I told my sister, "He said no more, so it's no more!" We have to be ready to hear his voice.

DECORATING THE TEMPLE

One might think or say, "Decorating is really easy; all you do is hang a decoration." Or one might ask, "What is so hard about decorating?" Believe me, even the simplest decorating may be difficult to do. When one is working for the Lord, one has a spiritual enemy (Satan). One doesn't even have to be working for the Lord to have this enemy.

> Your enemy the devil prowls around like a roaring lion looking for someone to devour."
>
> 1 Peter 5:8

> For our struggle is not against flesh and blood, but against the rulers, against the authorities, against the powers of this dark world and against the spiritual forces of evil in heavenly realms."
>
> Ephesians 6:12

An unseen world!

The enemy will try to attack and launch obstacles your way; that is his job. He may try by ensuring that you have car problems. He will try to create a hostile environment, cause confusion, and cause anger amongst department members.

Before one begins to decorate, I strongly recommend that everyone prays. Ask God that there be peace, creativity, energy, strength, and to send his angels to help. Be punctual in order to begin as scheduled. Based on experience, some will not arrive on time. As mentioned before, we have an enemy that will throw obstacles. I suggest that whoever is late should go to the altar and pray; no one should work unless they have prayed. Remember, work as a team, it brings power!

Regarding other departments, be considerate as one decorates the temple. Be careful that the decorations will not interfere with the instruments. If fresh flowers are to be used, ensure wiring will not get wet when watering flowers and plants. Ensure that the decorations will not interfere with the microphones, audio, visual, wiring, nor where the choir sits. Use common sense, respect every department.

While decorating the temple, take pictures of the members of the department as they decorate. Once completed, take pictures of all the decorations throughout the temple. Do this throughout the year for every holiday to document for your end of year report. You can also make a beautiful power point presentation and share it with everyone via the church website.

Decorating the temple entails that one pack tools, pack decorations, load and unload decorations, supplies, ladders, and ironing board from the house into the car. Load and unload decorations from the car into the temple. Climb ladders, hammer nails, bend, kneel, squat, measure, move the tall ladders from one place to the other. Remove decorations presently adorning the temple and then decorate for current holiday. Iron table cloths, flags, and/or panels one will hang as decorations. Clean and pick up any trash, conduct a final walk through to ensure tools, materials, supplies, etc. are not left behind. Then, when one is finished, one packs decorations, tools, load and unload decorations, supplies, ladders, ironing board from temple into the car. Once at home, unload all into the garage. I believe this is a lot of work for a fifty-six-year-old individual to do by herself. The first year I did the majority of the work. Most of the time throughout the year, my sister was unable to help me due to illness. The enemy always attacked her in that manner. Whenever she did help me, she would barely have enough strength to just do minimal decorating. There were times when I did hurt my back which required bed rest for three days or even a week after I decorated.

My Holy Father chose me to decorate his house of worship; I did it with all of my heart and without expecting anything in return. However, I learned a huge lesson. When one serves into the kingdom of God one will reap a harvest. He has blessed me enormously, my cup truly runneth over.

RECOGNIZE DEPARTMENT'S POTENTIAL AND IMPORTANCE

We need to remember that our focus should be on our Lord; to please him, be loyal, honor, and obey him. One must always remember that it is for him and him alone that one decorates. When we accomplish this, he will take care of the rest with his blessings. We won't have to worry whether the people like it, he will ensure that the decorations will please their spiritual eyes and the message He is conveying will be understood. He will bless us for our obedience.

As in Moses' time, God spoke to him and instructed him to build the tabernacle as per his instructions. God also specified every detail which consisted of measurements, materials, colors, designs, locations, and on how he wanted it built.

> Then have them make a sanctuary for me, and I will dwell among them. Make this

> tabernacle and all its furnishing exactly like the pattern I will show you.
>
> Exodus 25:8-9

After they pleased God, and all the details and aspects of the tabernacle were in place God dwelled amongst them as he said he would.

> So I will consecrate the Tent of Meeting and the altar and will consecrate Aaron and his sons to serve me as priests. Then I will dwell among the Israelites and be their God. They will know that I am the Lord their God, who brought them out of Egypt so that I might dwell among them. I am the Lord their God.
>
> Exodus 29:44-46

I learned that decorating his house of worship is extremely important. I feel very strongly that there is a need to respect and recognize the department's importance.

Although humbly, and with the budget my Lord gave me, my sister and I decorated the best we could for my Lord. I decorated the temple under his direction.

> And every skilled person to whom the Lord has given skill and ability to know how to carry out all the work of constructing the sanctuary are to do the work just as the Lord has commanded.
>
> Exodus 36:1

God selects the individuals that he wants to decorate his house of worship and will give them the skills necessary to accomplish the work at hand.

> He has filled them with skill to do all kinds of work as craftsmen, designers…
>
> Exodus 35:35

Many are called but few are chosen. You will also find that there aren't many that are willing to answer the call.

> And every skilled person to whom the Lord had given ability and who was willing to come and do the work.
>
> Exodus 36:2

DECORATIONS IN THE TEMPLE

As Director of the Ornamentation Department, I have learned an astonishingly valuable lesson about the decorations in the temple. Solely by the mere presence of God, the decorations are sanctified and anointed. I learned that God manifests through them. They have an enormous impact in the spiritual realm that we cannot even fathom. They have the capability to heal individuals as well as homes. He speaks through them as well: he uses images, symbols, and colors not solely to adorn his house but to also convey a visual message or to answer questions.

You might ask, how does one know when God is present? The tangible manifestation of the Holy Spirit might include falling, which is the most common; crying, trances, trembling, shaking, and others. This occurs due to the fact that our earthly bodies cannot withstand the presence of God.

Scriptures say that we must test all things to ensure that these are from God. We are exhorted to test the manifestations.

Test everything. Hold on to the good.

1 Thessalonians 5:21

Dear friends, do not believe every spirit, but test the spirits, to see whether they are of God, because many false prophets have gone out into the world.

1 John 4:1

The acts of the sinful nature are obvious: sexual immorality, impurity and debauchery; idolatry and witchcraft; hatred, discord, jealousy, fits of rage, selfish ambition, dissensions, factions and envy; drunkenness, orgies and the like.

Galatians 5:19

Does it honor God? Does it produce love or hatred? Does it lead you to truth, righteousness, joy, peace, patience, gentleness?

By their fruits you will recognize them… every good tree bears good fruit.

Matthew 7:16-17

But the fruit of the Spirit is love, joy, peace, patience, kindness, goodness, faithfulness, gentleness and self-control.

Galatians 5:22

There is a purpose for the decorations. For the reasons mentioned, I believe decorations should be respected and not be removed. I strongly suggest that there be communication between all departments. If a special event is to be held, such as a wedding, baptism, etc., ensure that the Ornamentation Department is contacted so that the decorations are not misplaced as they are removed and can be properly stored.

I decorated our Lord's house of worship under his direction, through words given to me by divine wisdom. He gave me the creativeness, the inspiration, the vision on how and what he wanted in his house.

The Lord instructed King Solomon to build and decorate the temple, which is a symbol of the New Jerusalem. Based on Bible scripture, my Holy Father likes color and beautiful things in his house.

> He paneled the main hall with pine and covered it with fine gold and decorated it with palm tree and chain designs.
>
> 2 Chronicles 3:5

> He adorned the temple with precious stones.
>
> 2 Chronicles 3:6

> The gold nails weighed fifty shekels.
>
> 2 Chronicles 3:9

> He made the curtain of blue, purple and crimson yarn and fine linen.
>
> 2 Chronicles 3:14

> The silver and gold and all the furnishings- and he placed them in the treasuries of God's temple.
>
> 2 Chronicles 3:14

> Gold for the gold work, silver for the silver, bronze for the bronze, iron for the iron and wood for the wood, as well as onyx for the settings, turquoise, stones of various colors, and all kinds of fine stone and marble.
>
> 1 Chronicles 29:2

The floral arrangements I made for every holiday were the best I could afford and as elegant and colorful as I could make them. Just as we like to decorate with seasonal decorations in our house, he also likes that. I used jewelry, silk birds, silk butterflies, fresh water pearls, faux (fake) pearls, crystal beads, feathers, tulle, and silk ribbon.

No matter how rich or how humble the Lord's house of worship is, the decorations should be the best one can afford and as elegant as can be. Decorations should not be "all right"; they should be as perfect as one can make them. Do not be satisfied with a decoration that is mediocre or that it looks okay. No, it has to be as perfect, as elegant as they can be. If it is good enough for your house, it should be better for his house. My Holy Father wants perfection. There will be times when you will be overwhelmed by your personal life and with your responsibility of decorating the Lord's house. Do not compromise; continue with perfection when it comes to decorating his house.

Make sure that you iron any panels, drapes, or table cloths you will be using as decorations. Would you hang wrinkled curtains in your home? Would you set a table with a wrinkled table cloth? Remember, you are decorating the Lord's house. It should be as elegant as can be. Just as you like your dwelling place to be comfortable, clean, pretty, pleasing to the eye, he also likes his house clean pretty and pleasing to the eye.

Adorn the church as a bride decorates the church for the marriage. My Holy Father wants his church decorated and ready. He's coming for the marriage soon, which is most commonly known as the rapture.

> Blessed are those who are invited to the wedding supper of the Lamb!
>
> Revelation 19:9

> We will all be changed in a flash, in the twinkling of an eye, at the last trumpet. For the trumpet will sound, the dead will be raised imperishable and we will be changed. For the perishable must clothe itself with the imperishable and the mortal with immortality.
>
> 1 Corinthians 15:51-53

Yes, the signs (earthquakes, famines, wars, rumors of wars) point that his return is forthcoming. However, the rapture must come first. Therefore, the rapture is imminent; it can happen without warning.

> For the Lord himself will come down from heaven, with a loud command, with the

> voice of the archangel and with the trumpet call of God, and the dead in Christ will rise first. After that, we who are still alive and are left will be caught up together with them in the clouds to meet the Lord in the air.
>
> 1 Thessalonians 4:16-17

As per Bible scripture, Jesus says that *He* is coming soon.

> Behold, I am coming soon!
>
> Revelation 22:7

> Behold, I am coming soon!
>
> Revelation 22:12

> Yes, I am coming soon.
>
> Revelation 22:20

When we take care of his house with the best decorations, he will also make sure that as his temple (the temple of the flesh) is dressed with the best clothes. He wants the best for his children.

> Do you not know that your body is a temple of the Holy Spirit, who is in you, whom you have received from God?
>
> 1 Corinthians 6:19

> For we are the temple of the living God.
>
> 2 Corinthians 6:16

The times that I have gone shopping for clothes, I've shopped at the most expensive shops. I have always found our clothes discounted fifty, seventy-five and up to eighty percent off regular price. One time I bought a skirt that I really liked at regular price, I felt guilty that I paid regular price; it wasn't much though. They had them in different colors and I wanted a couple more. I hadn't purchased clothes for quite some time and I had been offered a temporary job, so I needed a few things. I asked the sales lady if she had an idea as to when they would mark them down. She said they were not going to mark them down because they were selling very well. A few weeks later, my Holy Father prompted me to go to the store. To my surprise, they were marked down. Well, you guessed it, I bought a few more. My Holy Father will clothe you with the best. One reaps what one sows!

SUPERNATURAL CONNECTION/ COMMUNICATION

As mentioned before, I decorated our Lord's house of worship under his direction. He gave me the creativeness, inspiration, ingenuity, and the vision on how and what he wanted in his house.

The first time I realized that God conveys his message through the decorations was when I decorated for Spring 2009. He wanted me to decorate with butterflies. I said, butterflies, okay, but then I asked, "Why butterflies?" He later responded, so when people look at the butterflies, they will see what I can do with a worm, turn it into something beautiful.

For Easter 2009, my Holy Father wanted me to include a tombstone as one of the Easter decorations. I didn't have the slightest idea how to do that. My friend Mary and I went to Matamoros, Mexico to see if we could purchase one. We thought about having a piñata made into the shape of a tombstone. We didn't find one, and it was too expensive to have one made. She said it was too bad that her cousin was out of town and did not know when he would be back. Her cousin's work entails him to travel extensively. Easter was fast approaching and I didn't know how to go about making one. I told my Holy Father, "Well, I guess I won't have a tombstone." The following day, Mary called me to let me know that her cousin was in town. She said it was a miracle that he was in town and informed me that he was willing to make the tombstone.

He made a huge tombstone, and I asked him to spray paint the words "He is risen" on it in both English and Spanish.

Throughout the year I had been praying and asking my Holy Father to bring back to him those individuals who once knew him. It is my understanding that Mary's cousin had once been very involved with the church. He used to be in the drama department of his church and made all of the decorations for the dramas. He left the church many years ago, and this was the first time in a very long time that they were involved in doing something for the church.

The tombstone was supposed to have been used as a decoration. However, the Drama Department asked if it could be used in the Easter drama. I said sure. I was asked if they could spray paint over the words "He is risen." I said, "Well, you could try but that's how my Holy Father wanted it." Needless to say, the individual was unsuccessful.

Besides decorating for Easter, I also participated in the Easter drama as the angel. As I collected the accessories for my costume, my Holy Father instructed me to get a massive sword and to wear gloves. I have a lion head pendant, and he directed me to pin it on the middle finger of the glove. He said, so when they see you holding the sword they will see the lion, which symbolizes the lion of Judah. That evening, as part of my act, I was supposed to walk out. However, the door had been locked and was told that I had to stand in plain view throughout the play.

The most astonishing thing occurred after the play. The message the pastor delivered that evening was about the angel that God sent to the tomb, the tombstone and God's seal (lion) on his fist. As God as my witness, I had not had any communication whatsoever with the pastor. He is a very busy man and I do not bother him unless it is absolutely necessary.

Christmas 2009, my Holy Father spoke to my sister through a vision. He wanted a figurine of baby Jesus, Mary, and Joseph inside a metal see-through gift box. We found exactly what he wanted. I placed a picture frame with the words "The Gift" next to it. The drama department was presenting a Christmas drama. I was later informed that the drama was about "The Gift."

In January 2010, I presented a power point presentation to the congregation pertaining to the Ornamentation Department's decorations and accomplishments during 2009. One of the songs selected for the presentation was titled "*Despierta*" (Wake Up). After the presentation the pastor gave a short message, I could not believe it. His message was for us to wake up and spread the gospel. He kept repeating, Wake up! Wake up!

For Valentine's Day 2009 I decorated mainly with roses. But this year (2010) my Holy Father wanted me to decorate with hearts. So we did as he instructed. Again, to my surprise, the message that Sunday was "Guard your Heart."

Spring 2010 I decorated with large butterflies and attached some ribbons to each butterfly. At the end of the ribbon I attached the number twenty-five on it *(Misión Divina* is celebrating its twenty-fifth

Anniversary this year). I asked my Holy Father, "Why large butterflies?" He said, some of the congregation has matured, *Misión Divina* has grown.

Palm Sunday 2010—During the departmental meeting to discuss decorations for Palm Sunday, it was revealed to me that it had been the pastor's desire to have the temple filled with palm branches and lead the congregation into the temple. So, the day before we decorated, both men of the department went out and gathered a huge amount of palm branches. We decorated the temple with many, many palm branches. We laid palm branches beginning from the entrance to the church, then down on both isles all the way to the altar, and decorated the pillars. The temple looked beautiful. Sunday morning we surprised the pastor. I asked my Holy Father, "What do I tell the pastor?" He said, "Tell him this is something very sacred, this is not a show." We asked him to put the *Tallit* on and enter the temple by blowing the *Shofar*. I told him what my Holy Father instructed me to tell the pastor. (During the department meeting, we also discussed that perhaps the pastor could have a special blessing of the palm branches and have the congregation take them home.) In the course of the service that evening, we worshipped by waving the palm branches. To my surprise, the pastor instructed the congregation to raise the palm branches because God wanted to bless the branches and have us take them home. It is my understanding that in twenty-four years that the church has been in existence, Palm Sunday had never been celebrated in this manner. It turned out to be a very joyous celebration.

I wasn't sure what this meant, and the manner in which the enemy (Satan) attacks is by filling your mind with negative thoughts. The following day God spoke to me through the following scriptures from the Bible. This put my mind at ease; what transpired on Palm Sunday *was* what my Holy Father wanted.

> ...This day is sacred to our Lord. Do not grieve, for the joy of the Lord is your strength...Go out into the hill country and bring back branches from...palms...So the people went out and brought back branches...From the days of Joshua son of Nun until that day, the Israelites had not celebrated it like this. And their joy was very great.
>
> Nehemiah 8:10-17

Holy Supper 2010—Four days before we celebrated the Holy Supper, my Lord woke me up at 4:45 in the morning and instructed me to set a chair at the altar for him for this very Holy occasion. He told me to purchase some white fabric to decorate the chair with and that after the supper I was to go and pray for Mr. Juan Arias (Mary's dad). I was to cover Mr. Arias from head to toe with the white fabric. (Note: Mr. Arias had been stricken with a stroke and was being fed through a tube that had been inserted in his stomach. He was unable to eat on account of the stroke; it had left him paralyzed and unable to speak as well.) It was late when we left the church. However, I called Mary to inform her about what my Holy Father had instructed me to do. She called the rehabilitation center and the night nurse did not allow me to go pray for him. We celebrated Holy Supper on Thursday so it was Holy Friday when I went to pray for Mr. Arias.

I asked my Holy Father, "What do I say?" He reminded me of the scripture (Acts 11:5-10) where

Peter in a trance saw a vision. He saw a large sheet being let down from heaven by its four corners and God told him not to call anything impure that God has made clean. I asked Mrs. Arias if she remembered about Peter's vision and about not calling anything impure that God has made clean. She said yes. I anointed and covered Mr. Arias as my Holy Father instructed me to do, from head to toe, and prayed over him. As I began to pray, our Lord's presence was felt in the room. I prayed that just as Jesus rose from the dead, Mr. Arias would rise from that bed. I prayed that God cleanse Mr. Arias from the impurities, that what God has cleansed it will not be impure.

Based on what Mrs. Arias was going through (she had also been diagnosed with skin cancer), I felt in my heart to anoint her, and partially place the white material on her and pray for her. The following day Mary called me to let me know that her father was talking. He began gaining strength and started walking a bit more each day. I have been informed that Mrs. Arias is now healed from the skin cancer doctors had diagnosed her with. All the glory to our Almighty God!

For the longest time I could not figure out what all this meant. It took me quite some time before I realized my Holy Father wants a visual as well as an audible message. I learned that there *is* a supernatural connection/communication. This only proves that he does speak to us as his word says and the decorations do have healing powers.

Therefore, look beyond the face value of a decoration; ask our Lord for discernment. It is not just about decorating or adorning his house of worship, but to also fulfill its purpose of visually conveying his message, answering your questions, and using them for healing.

PICTURES

During the course of the year I took pictures of all the decorations we used to decorate the Temple with. I do this for posterity and to compile for the end of the year power point presentation. I would like to share some pictures I took in 2009 and 2010. If you look closely you will see orbs on picture number five, number ten and number thirteen.

As I mentioned before, I played the part of the angel for the Easter drama in 2009. If you will note on picture number five you will see a huge orb right above the sword. I believe this is the supernatural manifestation of the Holy Spirit.

On Palm Sunday 2010 during praise and worship, my Holy Father told me to take a picture. If you look closely at picture number ten you will see many, many orbs.

In Mary Lucio's testimony, she writes about how her little daughter had prayed and asked God to send his angels to protect her father at work. If you look at picture number thirteen you will see many orbs.

On the author picture you will see an orb above my shoulder. Before we began the photo shoot we prayed. I asked God that he allow his angels to appear in the picture. My sister took about twenty-one pictures. This is the only picture which an orb this size appears.

I have many pictures that I have taken at home, at church, at special functions and at family gatherings where these orbs appear. As I mentioned before, prior to decorating the Temple for any occasion I always pray that God send his angels to protect us. In some of the pictures that I have, there are orbs by the individuals as they decorate the church. There are orbs by the ladder when an individual is on the ladder decorating. There is one picture that I took at church where you can actually see the image of a lion's face (the lion of Judah) on the orb. You can view these pictures in facebook. Based on my personal experience and personal relationship with God, I humbly believe that these supernatural orbs are angels and/or the Holy Spirit. I acknowledge that Satan will try to deceive us, but I doubt it very seriously that on all these occasions he would want to give God all the honor and glory.

> So whatever I say is just what the Father has told me to say.
>
> John 12:50

> These words you hear are not my own; they belong to the Father…
>
> John 14:24

> The angel of the Lord encamps around those who fear him, and he delivers them.
>
> Psalm 34:7

For he will command his angels concerning you to guard you in all your ways.

Psalm 91:11

for it is written: He will command his angels concerning you...

Matthew 4:6

For it is written: He will command his angels concerning you to guard you carefully.

Luke 4:10

In the last days, God says,...I will show wonders in the heaven above and signs on the earth...

Acts 2:17,19

Therefore I glory in Christ Jesus in my service to God. I will not venture to speak of anything except what Christ has accomplished through me in leading the Gentiles to obey God by what I have said and done— by the power of signs and miracles through the power of the Spirit...

Romans 15:17-19

Spring 2009 butterflies

Mary & cousin working on tombstone

Easter 2009 Tombstone "He is Risen"

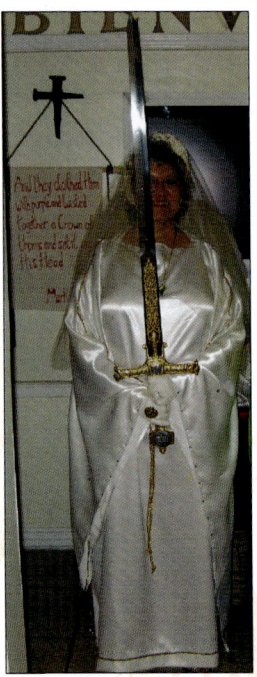

Massive sword/Lion of Judah ring

Orb by the Sword Easter 2009

The Gift- Christmas 2009

Valentines 2010 - hearts

Spring 2010 – large butterfly

Palm Sunday 2010 – palms in entrance to church

Palm Sunday 2010 - congregation worshiping at church

Holy Supper 2010-Chair for Jesus with white material

Holy Supper 2010

Angels around Mary's husband while at work

Zárate-Muñiz in Jerusalem

Rainbow over face

SPIRITUAL DECORATIONS

The materials in the New Jerusalem:

> The wall was made of jasper, and the city of pure gold, as pure as glass. The foundations of the city walls were decorated with every kind of precious stone. The first foundation was jasper, the second, sapphire, the third, chalcedony, the fourth, emerald, the fifth, sardonyx, the sixth, carnelian, the seventh, chrysolite; the eighth beryl, the ninth, topaz; the tenth, chrysoprase, the eleventh, jacinth; the twelfth, amethyst. The twelve gates were twelve pearls; each gate made of a single pearl. The great street of the city was of pure gold; like transparent glass.
>
> Revelation 21:18-20

One day I received a phone call from Mary, she wanted to share a vision God had given to her. She had been researching an online Jewish encyclopedia that day. She was reading a portion where it talked about the tabernacle and stated that it had a chair specifically for

Elijah. The following is what transpired: She immediately asked God regarding the chair, "If the tabernacle is a sacred place, why are you decorating it with Elijah's presence in it? How do you decorate your heaven?" (If you do know the story of Elijah it probably just made perfect sense as to why the chair was there.) In God's great mercy, he responded to her, "There is a purpose for everything in his path. It is my will and pleasure to decorate my heaven with those who have been washed with the blood of the Lamb which is Jesus, who obey me and have the fruits of the spirit within them. My final masterpiece will be when I return and bring with me all of those who have been redeemed by Jesus to heaven and if you want to be part of my beautiful décor up in my palace you know what you have to do!"

God Wants You for His Kingdom

God wants you to be his gem, his celestial property, to be a part of his treasure.

> 'They will be mine,' says the Lord Almighty, 'in the day when I make up my treasured possession...'
>
> Malachi 3:17

> Now if you obey me fully and keep my covenant, then out of all nations you will be my treasured possession.
>
> Exodus 19:5

Come and be a crown in his hand.

> You will be a crown of splendor in the Lord's hand, a royal diadem in the hand of your God.
>
> Isaiah 62:3

Come and be a part of his decoration in his kingdom. God is waiting on you. Open your heart to Jesus Christ; believe, accept Jesus Christ as your Lord and Savior.

To become a part of his treasure; a decoration in his kingdom, pray the following prayer to be born again (a spiritual birth):

> In reply Jesus declared, 'I tell you the truth, no one can see the kingdom of God unless he is born again.'
>
> John 3:3

> *"God, forgive me for my sins, come into my life.*
> *I accept you as my Lord and Savior.*
> *I believe that Jesus is your son, that he was crucified, that he died for my sins,*
> *and that he arose from the dead.*
> *And now I am born again.*
> *In Jesus name I pray, amen!"*

If you have prayed this prayer with a sincere heart, congratulations; you are now born again.

There is rejoicing in heaven because you have repented and accepted Jesus as your Savior.

Jesus said in Luke 15:7, "I tell you that in the same way there will be more rejoicing in heaven over one sinner who repents..."

God has forgiven your sins and remembers them no more.

> I, even I am he who blots out your transgressions...
>
> Isaiah 43:25

> Blessed is he whose transgressions are forgiven, whose sins are covered. Blessed is the man whose sin the Lord does not count against him and in whose spirit is no deceit.
>
> Psalm 32:1-2

> As far as the east is from the west, so far has he removed our transgressions from us.
>
> Psalm 103:12

> And hurl all our iniquities into the depths of the sea.
>
> Micah 7:19

When one accepts Jesus, the Holy Spirit lives within one. This is the wisest decision you have ever made. To continue your walk with Jesus, read the Bible so that you won't be deceived. Attend a Bible-based church that preaches the truth. You ask, "How would I know which church preaches the truth?" Simple, ask God to lead you to a church that preaches the truth; he will. I know, based on my personal experience, I always wanted a church that preached the truth. God answered my prayers. He led me to *Misión Divina*.

God loves us immensely that it was love that compelled him to save us from sin. Love compelled God to send his son to die for us; not for the angels, but for us sinners! He loves us when we are sinners, but when we are born again he loves us even more; our former sins are forgotten.

> Blessed is he whose transgressions are forgiven, whose sins are covered. Blessed is the man whose sin the Lord does not count against him and in whose spirit is no deceit.
>
> Psalm 32:1-2

As his temple, he will clothe us and adorn us in the spiritual realm. The decorations and glow of the Spirit are what people will see in you. The glorious splendor of our Holy Father's glory, radiance, and grace will be projected through you. He will give us splendor and radiance, garments of salvation, a robe of righteousness, a crown of love, compassion, and beauty; necklace of discernment and sound judgment, and knowledge, a rare jewel.

1. God's glory, radiance, splendor.

> Do you not know that your body is a temple of the Holy Spirit, who is in you, whom you have received from God?
>
> 1 Corinthians 6:19

> For we are the temple of the living God.
>
> 2 Corinthians 6:16

> He has endowed you with splendor.
>
> Isaiah 60:9

Moses covered with the Glory of God—

> He was not aware that his face was radiant…
>
> Exodus 34:29

God's glory shone through the face of Stephen—

> … Looked intently at Stephen, and they saw that his face was like the face of an angel.
>
> Acts 6:15

2. Garments of salvation and a robe of righteousness.

> … For He has clothed me with garments of salvation and arrayed me in a robe of righteousness, as a bridegroom adorns his head like a priest, and as a bride adorns herself with her jewels.
>
> Isaiah 61:10

3. Crown of love, compassion, beauty, and splendor.

> … Crowns you with love and compassion.
>
> Psalm 103:4

...To bestow on them a crown of beauty.

> Isaiah 61:3

...Your inner self, the unfading beauty of a gentle and quiet spirit, which is of great worth in God's sight.

> 1 Peter 3:4

Gray hair is a crown of splendor; it is attained by a righteous life.

> Proverbs 16:31

4. Necklace—sound judgment and discernment, like a beautiful necklace.

Preserve sound judgment and discernment...they will be life for you, an ornament to grace your neck.

> Proverbs 3:21,22

5. Rare jewel.

Lips that speak knowledge are a rare jewel.

> Proverbs 20:15

The earth is full of his gems—rubies, emeralds, diamonds, amethysts and more, all waiting to be extracted and made beautiful. God has chosen us as his gem. When God picks us and we accept Jesus as our Lord and Savior with a sincere heart, we are born again (a spiritual birth). So when we are extracted from the secular world, we are like the gems when they are first extracted from the earth; they are not pretty. They have rough edges, are filthy, full of dirt and mud (that is our sins such as adultery, gambling, fornication, worship of idols, pride, lust, cussing, lying, drugs, abortions, etc.). Thus, he has to purify us. We will need to go through a purifying process in order to cleanse us. The purifying process may involve going through the grinding wheel, polishing, fire, cutting, filing, and so on. Depending on the type and extent of the treatment or process can affect the value of the stone. We will be refined by the fire, polishing, filing and so forth. The grinding, polishing, filing, and fire, are the trials and tribulations we face, such as the death of a loved one, either by natural causes or suicide, cancer, depression, and so on. The storms in our lives will smooth our rough edges so that we may become a reflection of him. He loves us. He will provide for us and give us the peace we need to endure. He will never leave us!

> And surely I am with you always, to the very end of age.
>
> Matthew 28:20

God is the jeweler of jewelers. Therefore, if we endure, we will surpass the elegance we need so that he will adorn his kingdom with us. Such are the storms in our lives!

TESTIMONIES
Dahlia Zárate-Muñiz: Why God led me to Misión Divina

The following is my testimony of the storms I was experiencing when my Holy Father led me to *Iglesia Misión Divina Centrál*. He knew more storms were coming my way, and he blessed me enormously by leading me to *Misión Divina*. It was my choice whether I would have faith and trust him.

I chose to have faith and to trust him; as a result I have seen and experienced many miracles and wonders since.

> Blessed is the man that trusts in him.
>
> Psalm 34:8

> He will make your righteousness shine like the dawn.
>
> Psalm 37:6

Your righteousness: that is, the prosperity and well-being that God will bestow in accordance with your faithful reliance on him.

The Art of Decoration

> ...but to Put their hope in God, who richly provides us with everything for our enjoyment.
>
> 1 Timothy 6:17

> Do not worry about your life, what you will eat or drink; or about your body what you will wear...look at the birds of the air, they do not sow or reap...yet your heavenly Father feeds them. Are you not much more valuable than they?
>
> Matthew 6:25-33

> And my God will meet all your needs according to his glorious riches in Christ Jesus
>
> Philippians 4:19

I was experiencing several storms, but by God's mercy and grace, I did not go insane. I will briefly share the storms I was living through.

I was caring for my ninety-four year old father, whose health was rapidly deteriorating. He was hospitalized and was suffering from congestive heart failure. At the same time, I needed to drive my husband to the Veterans Hospital in San Antonio, Texas, which is about a four-hour drive north from where we live. My husband's cancer had invaded his liver. My sister, a diabetic, was very ill in the hospital suffering from a very serious and deadly infection.

My husband began his chemotherapy treatments. My father was too ill for me to give him the quality care he needed at home. As a result, I had to place him in a nursing home, and the guilt feelings were plaguing me. My father passed away a couple of months later. I was his care giver; he had lived with us, so I was the one that made all the funeral arrangements.

I had been oppressed, harassed, and discriminated at my place of employment by my supervisors. We needed the income and I needed the health insurance, so I could not afford to leave my employment. However, several months later I was laid off from work; consequently my husband began working fulltime. I became very ill and needed to have surgery to remove my gall bladder.

Again, my husband was re-diagnosed with cancer on his liver. He began his chemotherapy treatments a month later. I was about to literally go crazy; one more minute and I believe I would have gone insane. I felt no peace, no peace, a horrible emptiness, as if I were suffocating. I had not mentioned anything to any one, not even my husband. He was going through enough. I called my cousin Cookie, and I told him I could not take it anymore. I didn't know what to do. I asked him to please pray for me. He came over and prayed for me. Divine intervention occurred instantly. I felt so much peace, peace that I had not felt in months. A huge weight lifted off my shoulders. I felt peace flow throughout my body. At that point, I totally submitted myself to God.

Faith Activates Miracles

I began reading the scriptures and listening to the Christian channels on television. I learned that we can go boldly to God's throne. The *first miracle* occurred when my husband was taking chemo the second time. He was smoking, and I told him he was defeating the purpose. He had tried to quit several times before by using the patch, but had been unsuccessful every time. One evening he was outside smoking and I was in my room. I remembered the scriptures in the Bible:

> Ask and it will be given to you … For everyone who asks receives.
>
> Matthew 7:7-8

I remembered that one can boldly approach God's throne and quote scripture, or remind God what his word says.

> Let us then approach the throne of grace with confidence, so that we may receive mercy and find grace to help us in our time of need.
>
> Hebrews 4:16

I decided I would take that approach. This was my prayer that evening: "God, you say that if we ask, it will be given to you. So I am asking, help my husband stop smoking, in Jesus name, amen." I went outside and told my husband to ask God to help him stop smoking. He did ask God. After fifty-four years of smoking, my husband stopped smoking the following day. He hasn't smoked since. This has been three years now.

I thank my Holy Father for leading us to *Misión Divina*. We had the support of the pastor and the intercessors who were praying for us.

My husband's chemotherapy treatments did not work; therefore, he needed to have major surgery. My husband was seventy-three years old at that time and the doctors did not give him much of a chance to live. Death was knocking at my husband's door. The *second miracle* occurred. I said to my Holy Father, I am asking that you save my husbands' life. He gave me the scriptures to give my husband. My husband prayed and read all the scriptures pertaining to healing every night. God also gave me Bible scripture and prayer to rebuke death. God is so merciful; my husband survived the surgery. God also gave me the strength and energy to take care of my husband. The first night after my husband was released from the hospital; he had a fever all night. I went without sleep for thirty three hours straight but I felt strong and was alert.

As we were preparing for our trip back to San Antonio for my husband's surgery we had to euthanize our pet cat of 16 years. Her kidneys had begun to fail, so, a couple of days before we left to San Antonio we had our cat put to sleep. This didn't help my husband much, he loved that cat. It was hard on him when we returned home after his surgery, I could see it in his eyes that he missed his cat very much. Every time we would return from San Antonio, his cat was always there to greet him. This time she wasn't there for him.

As a result of my being laid off, I asked another cousin, who is a very prominent attorney, if he would review my case. I talked to him via the telephone the day before we left for San Antonio. After researching my case, he agreed that there had been a huge injustice made against me. However, he refused to help me. Being fully aware of my husband's condition and our financial situation, he wanted a huge amount of money up front. I thanked him, said "God Bless you," and I hung up the phone. The enemy began to bombard my mind; I didn't know whether I'd be back a widow, or whether we'd be back and be out on the streets. I didn't know how I would take care of my husband. I got on my knees and I prayed. I surrendered it all to my Holy Father.

My Holy Father revealed to me that persons were praying against me. I also found out through an acquaintance that witchcraft was being done against me.

Our income was less than our expenses, and my retirement funds were quickly depleting. As a result of all that transpired, it was a hardship for us to continue to pay certain bills, so we filed bankruptcy.

I didn't have medical nor dental insurance. I got physically ill again and needed medical attention.

After all this, a huge tragedy occurred. A very close member of the family was very ill, consequently, he took his own life. It pierced my soul and spirit; such immense pain.

It has been a whirlwind, an emotional roller coaster, but I thank my Holy Father for all that I have been through. I learned that without him I am nothing. If I had not experienced all this turmoil, I never would have discovered how much he truly loves me.

I submitted myself to him and chose to obey the Word of God, follow the righteous path, honor him, put him first, do his will, and please him. It is true that when one delights in the Lord, and is obedient, it produces divine rewards. If you do the natural, God will do the supernatural.

> Delight yourself in the Lord and he will give you the desires of your heart.
>
> Psalm 37:4

Because I surrendered to him, he has blessed me with peace, sanity, my husband, good health, a roof over my head, food on my table, clothes on my back, and am financially stable.

God has manifested himself to me through gold dust on my hands several times. The first time was in the year 2007. Again in March 2009, the gold appeared on my hands and remained for about two days. Another time in 2009, I recall driving my husband to San Antonio, Texas for a follow up with the doctors at the veteran's hospital; gold dust appeared on my clothes.

When I went to Israel, I had my picture taken on the Mount of Beatitudes, and God's glory manifested; there is a rainbow over my face.

He has also blessed me with five silver fillings in my teeth. In the year 2000, David Herzog wrote a book *Mysteries of the Glory Unveiled,* and he talks about signs and wonders. One sign and wonder would be that God would turn old fillings to silver and some in the shape of a cross or a dove. On July 2008, my Holy Father turned my old darkened fillings to silver fillings, and one is in the shape of a dove.

On September 2009 we had a revival at our church. The guest speaker asked if there was anyone that wanted to grow. I went up to the altar, and in front of the congregation he spoke to my legs to grow. My legs stretched and literally grew two inches.

Our income is less than our expenses. If I didn't believe, my husband and I would be literally out on the streets, insane, or perhaps six feet under.

Believe, believe in God's promises. Believe in his word. One may read the Bible, know the scriptures, memorize his word, and preach the gospel. However, it's of no use if one does not put into action what the scripture says. Walk the righteous path as he commands, and you will be blessed.

> Do not worry about your life, what you will eat or drink; or about your body what you will wear...look at the birds of the air, they do not sow or reap...yet your heavenly Father feeds them. Are you not much more valuable than they?
>
> Matthew 6:25-33

> Do not conform any longer to the pattern of this world, but be transformed by the renewing of your mind.
>
> Romans 12:2

> And my God will meet all your needs according to his glorious riches in Christ Jesus.
>
> Philippians 4:19

> …But to put their hope in God, who richly provides us with everything for our enjoyment.
>
> 1 Timothy 6:17

> And God is able to make all grace abound to you, so that in all things at all times, having all that you need…
>
> 2 Corinthians 9:8

I remember this one time when my husband and I were driving home from Harlingen. He was hungry and he asked me if I had any money. He said he didn't have much, he only had three cents. I said, "Well, let me look in my purse." After I counted my money, I responded, "I'm rich; I have five cents."

> The tongue has the power of life and death, and those who love it will eat its fruit.
>
> Proverbs 18:21

If you speak abundance, abundance you will have. If you say that you're always sick, then you will always be sick. Words don't have jurisdiction on earth until you speak them. Words are powerful sources, so be careful what you say; quit speaking negatively. This is a very serious matter; not all Christians are aware of this. Although I was brought up as a Christian, I didn't know this. I found out when I began my relationship with God and learned about his ways. So beware of what comes out of your mouth.

Your mind competes with your faith; obey with your heart; trust with your heart not your logic. Act by faith, faith produces miracles, divine supernatural miracles. God acts on faith!

> …if you have faith as small as a mustard seed, you can say to this mountain, "Move from here to there and it will move, Nothing will be impossible for you.
>
> Matthew 17:20

A Pleasing Offering to God

We can all agree that God surely works in mysterious ways. Throughout my first year at *Misión Divina* I noticed that no one decorated the temple. Based on my relationship with my Holy Father, I now believe this was all in his plan. In order for me to write this book, I had to have experienced all that transpired and be of benefit to many. When I was offered the position, I was informed that the temple had been decorated, but for some reason it hadn't been done that year.

It all started when I noticed no one decorated the temple and Christmas was approaching. I wanted my Holy Father's house to look pretty for Christmas. I thought, *Maybe I could make some floral arrangements for Christmas.* However, our bills were more than our income and we didn't have funds to buy supplies and material to make floral arrangements. We had some payments that were due. I looked at our checkbook and I contemplated, *Either I pay the bill or I buy the supplies I need for the decorations.* It was an either/or situation.

I opted to buy the materials and supplies to make the floral arrangements for the temple. I thought to myself, *I'll figure something out later. I'll go pawn some of my jewelry.* I went shopping and spent the money that was to be used to pay the bill.

I was not expecting anything in return; the thought hadn't even entered my mind. To my surprise, the following day I was approved for unemployment benefits. I was very happy. I called my husband at work to let him know about how God had blessed us. Then the following day, to our huge surprise, we were blessed with ten thousand dollars; my jaw just dropped. I began to cry. All I wanted was to make my Holy Father's house look pretty for Christmas. It is so true that if one puts God first he will bless us. God blesses those that give from the heart, a cheerful heart.

God put in pastor's heart that I direct the department. The following January, Pastor Izaguirre offered me the position as the Director of Ornamentation Department.

Praying to God

When asking God for something, be specific and ask with expectations. Throughout the year I had been praying to my Holy Father and asking him to take me to Israel. I asked him that I wanted to go before the end of the year. It went on all through August. Well, he answered my prayers. We were blessed with the ten thousand dollars. That was more than enough for the trip. But my Holy Father told me, if you want to go you need to go now. I told my husband that my

Holy Father told me that I needed to go now. I made all the travel arrangements and went the first week in November. About two weeks later after I returned home, war broke out in Gaza.

If you put God first in all that you do and are obedient to him, he will give you the desires of your heart.

> May he give you the desire of your heart.
>
> Psalm 20:4

He will bless you abundantly. His word is true.
Believe for the impossible.

> Do not conform any longer to the pattern of this world, but be transformed by the renewing of your mind...
>
> Romans 12:2

Miracles and Wonders

Regarding the finances for the department, I found myself in a predicament. With all due respect, I will share my personal experience pertaining to finances. I did not comprehend the enormous impact our worship has in the spiritual realm. I acknowledge that many times we attend church, we pray, we sing, but we don't realize what we are actually doing. We have been taught rituals, and not to actually establish a personal relationship with God.

When I was offered the director position, I was informed that I needed to raise funds to sustain the department. The norm for the departments is to have an activity, such as selling hot dogs, dinner plates, cupcakes, etc. after the service. The procedure was that I had to leave before the service was over so that I could prepare the table outside the church. I was not comfortable with that. I told the person that I refused to leave my Holy Father's presence to go outside and sell. The person said, "That's all right you can have someone else do that for you and you can join them after the service." I responded, "No, I would never ask anyone to leave my Holy Father's presence, either."

Something within me would tell me no, that is not right. My friend tried to convince me that it was all right; it was for the Lord's house. But, I said "No, no, no, I refuse to leave my Holy Father's presence. I don't feel it is right."

I prayed to my Holy Father; I asked him, "What do I do? I don't want to leave your presence, I don't know how to cook and I am not a salesperson." My Holy Father's response was for me not to ask men for money, but to ask him.

The first time I asked my Holy Father for money was for Valentine's Day. The holiday was fast approaching. I said, okay, my Holy Father, I need money to buy the supplies for Valentine's Day. Well, it was either that same day or the day after, my husband came home after work and said, here, honey, so and so came by and gave me a thousand dollars to help me. (My husband has very many friends and acquaintances that care and love him. They all knew about his cancer and the situation in which we were in.) They were all one hundred dollar bills. My jaw just dropped. Later I asked my Holy Father, "How much do I spend from this?"

He said, "One hundred dollars."

This went on all year for every holiday. When a holiday was approaching, I would ask my Holy Father for money. It was either that same day or the following that my husband would come home after work and say, "Here, honey, so and so gave me a thousand dollars." My hands were overflowing with money, always with hundred dollar bills.

Every time we are blessed financially, we are obedient and give our tithes and offerings to God without fail.

> Honor the Lord with your wealth, with the first fruits of all your crops; then your barns will be filled to overflowing.
>
> Proverbs 3:9,10

> A tithe of everything from the land whether grain from the soil or fruit from the trees, belongs to the Lord; it is holy to the Lord.
>
> Leviticus 27:30

We don't want to rob the ten percent that belongs to the Lord. When you tithe you are giving reverence to God. He will bless you when you give reverence to him. For those who bring their tithes and offerings, God promises to pour out more blessing than they have room for. He has opened the gates of heaven to us as his word says.

> …But you ask, 'How do we rob you?' 'In tithes and offerings. You are under a curse— the whole nation of you because you are rob-

> bing me…Test me in this,' says the Lord Almighty, 'and see if I will not throw open the floodgates of heaven and pour out so much blessing that you will not have room enough for it.'
>
> Malachi 3:8-10

If you don't believe me, test him as he says to do so. Give him an opportunity; just as you would want to be given an opportunity.

When we first began tithing, we had to choose whether we would pay our bills or tithe. We chose to tithe; we now give more than ten percent. The more you give, the more God will bless you. We always have all that we need. We lack for nothing!

With the funds provided, I always purchased the best silk flowers, fresh flowers, ornaments, materials, fabrics, ribbons, crystal trays, etc. After all, it is for his house. I always found the supplies, materials, etc. at a discount, always fifty, sixty, even up to eighty percent off. He will lead you to the mark down sales. I bought a beautiful table cloth for Holy Supper: the asking price was two hundred and fifty and was marked down to fifty dollars. He will always supply you with all you need to decorate his house of worship. Pray and ask him to supply you with what you need at a mark down price. He will!

My Holy Father did all this because I refused to leave his presence. That is the power of worship and prayer. All God wants from us is to seek him, humble ourselves before him, love him, praise him, be obedient, and have faith in him.

I put my Holy Father first, because I put him first in all that I do and humbled myself before him; he has blessed me ever since in abundance.

Maria de la Luz Arias-Lucio

In 1988 I became an active member in a church in Brownsville, Texas, USA. I remember those years so dearly. I was sure that if I lived I would work for my God, and if I died I would be rejoicing in his presence. It is a great security in the life of every true Christian. Every day I would enjoy fasting, praying, and talking about God's love to others. I was participating in all types of activities within my church. I was chosen to be a teacher assistant for the morning service, and I soon got trained to be a teacher for the children's program. It was an honor to serve God with all my heart and be open to his voice and will. On special occasions I enjoyed participating in dramas and commenced the first part of the service singing various gospel songs with the congregation. I loved to attend youth conferences and campaigns. Usually on the days our church did not have service we would either visit other temples, pass out flyers or pamphlets, or visit our local juveniles in jail to preach the word of God unto them in company of our sister-in-Christ Julia Fuentes. My relationship with our Lord was supreme and sweet.

Spiritual World

We know a supernatural world exists. However, we have to learn to discern spirits. In fact, angels and demons are as real as the air we breathe. Though I could never see them, I could feel when they were around or near me. When fasting, I used to ask God to wake me up at 6:00 a.m. Every morning on those days, I believe that angels would wake me up in the morning. Sometimes I would either hear a loud bang on the window as if a rock had been thrown at it. As soon as I would check the time, the clock marked 6:00 a.m. On occasions my Holy Father used to call me by my name in the mornings until I woke up. Unfortunately, Satan doesn't sleep, and many times demons would bother me in dreams when praying or as I was working for our Lord. I could feel the tension and negative vibes around me. Quickly I would rebuke them in the name of Jesus.

My parents knew about Jesus and the blessings they had received in their lives in the past. However, they were in great need of a revival in their lives. There was a strong desire in my heart for my parents to not only accept Jesus but to attend church. It constantly boggled my mind, until one day on September 4, 1992, God spoke to me and said that he had everything under control and that I was not to worry about my family anymore. At that time I gave it all to Jesus.

My Spiritual Death

In the year 1995 my cousin was the president for the youth in the church. Ms. Julia Fuentes was the teacher, and I was her assistant for the Sunday school. Our loving brother Paco Gonzalez was my youth teacher at that time and his teachings were and will always be a huge blessing in my life. He not only preached the Word, but also lived it.

During this same year, close to Mother's Day my spirit was murdered along with all my joy. Sadly, when as a Christian, if your vision is not all on God but on men, things can go very wrong. The youth had gathered to practice a Mother's Day gospel song named *"Ella Es Mi Madre"* (she is my mother), which is a solemn song. The youth had been practicing in church since morning and it was getting late. New youth had joined the church and we had a new pastor.

The new church group's objective that day was to take the song we had been practicing and convert the notes of the song to a hard rock type. My cousin and I tried to participate. However, God put in our hearts that there was something wrong in the way things were being handled. When you walk in God's path it is very important to know how to discern and understand when God speaks to you.

Godly Jealousy

That day we both felt that what we were doing did not please God and we understood that he did not want that on his altar. Throughout the world, these days, many do not know that there is a certain type of spiritual jealousy (godly jealousy) that exists; just as the one that moved Jesus as he entered the temple.

> When it was almost time for the Jewish Passover, Jesus went up to Jerusalem. In the temple courts he found men selling cattle, sheep, and doves, and others sitting at tables exchanging money. So he made a whip out of cords, and drove all from the temple area, both sheep and cattle; he scattered the coins

> of the money changers and overturned their tables. To those who sold doves he said, "Get these out of here! How dare you turn my Father's house into a market!
>
> John 2:13-16

Worship, praise, and honor belong only to God, because only he is worthy to receive it.

That is why his anger is justified when what is offered to God is not pure or pleasing to him. Apostle Paul talks to us about this:

> I am jealous for you with a godly jealousy. I promised you to one husband, to Christ, so that I might present you as a pure virgin to him.
>
> 2 Corinthians 11:2

What we offer or the manner in which we do the things might not be pleasing to God.

> In the course of time Cain brought some of the fruits of the soil as an offering to the Lord. But Abel brought fat portions from some of the firstborn of his flock. The Lord looked with favor on Abel and his offering, but on Cain and his offering he did not look with favor. So Cain was very angry, and his face was downcast. Then the Lord said to Cain, "Why are you angry? Why is your face downcast? If you do what is right, will you not be accepted? But if you do not do what is right, sin is crouching at your door; it desires to have you, but you must master it.
>
> Genesis 4:3-6

Unfortunately, what is not known or what is not comprehended will always be criticized. On that occasion we chose to hear God's voice and we cordially addressed it to the youth. We apologized to them; we felt that this was not appropriate and that we were not going to participate with what they were doing.

Incomprehension Unleashed

We were really astonished at the reaction and attitude that some of them took regarding that day. They criticized our decision and they began to attack with such words as "you think you're real holy"; some of the new members began to cuss. They had just been playing at the altar. After that came the worst for us. A band member said, "As for us leave, we don't need you."

Note: For reasons such as these, we need to be jealous (godly jealousy) about what is done, or what is permitted to happen on God's altar.

My cousin burst out crying and couldn't take it anymore and preferred to leave on foot.

We didn't live near the church. We had come in the church van, and the pastor still hadn't arrived. I didn't let her leave by herself. There was only one youth that asked us not to leave. I believe he was the only one that felt something in his heart about what had just happened. I explained to him that I could not let my cousin leave by herself at night; he understood.

That night we walked a bit toward a supermarket that was close by. We called my cousin Juan from there so that he could pick us up. After a few minutes, we saw the pastor's car approach us. He asked if someone was coming for us. We said yes and he left. After a while they came for us.

This day was a day like no other and it is not easy for me to write about, but God has a time. I believe the time has come for my testimony to come afloat. I rebuke any spirit of resentment and negativity, be gone, in Jesus's name! And I now begin to write in the name of the Father, the Son, and the Holy Spirit. Amen! Let this serve as testimony to many, and I have faith that my experience will help others be more protective of their spiritual life.

The Meeting: A Dark and Grey Afternoon

The very next day we were told the pastor was going to have a formal meeting with the youth, deacons, and all church officials. We thought that was the best thing to do for we believed the meeting was to reconcile the youth, be guided with God's word, and receive encouragement to move forward. We were pleased by this thought. The Bible teaches us about forgiveness in:

> Brothers, if someone is caught in a sin, you who are spiritual should restore him gently. But watch yourself, or you also may be tempted.
>
> Galatians 6:1

> And when you stand praying, if you hold anything against anyone, forgive him, so that your Father in heaven may forgive you your sins.
>
> Mark 11:25,26

> For if you forgive men when they sin against you, your heavenly Father will also forgive you.
>
> Matthew 6:14

> Then came Peter to him, and said, 'Lord, how oft shall my brother sin against me, and I forgive him. Till seven times?' Jesus saith unto him, 'I say not unto thee, until seven times but, until seventy times seven.'
>
> Matthew 18:21,22 (KJV)

Unfortunately, my cousin was deeply hurt and she made the wrong decision to leave her position as Youth President. I really did not agree with her decision, for God had placed her there, not men. The meeting took place at church in the afternoon.

During the meeting, the pastor, his wife, youth, deacons, and church officials were in the meeting. Other church members were right outside in the temple's hallway.

Our heart was pierced when the pastor commenced the meeting by saying we are here to clarify and see who was at fault about what happened. Again we were attacked by the enemy. We never expected something like this. The pastor was in front of the pulpit and his wife beside him. I really never comprehended the posture, the anger, and annoyance of the pastors' wife that afternoon. For an instant I tried, but their daughters and a son of other families or friends of theirs were involved in what had transpired. Her anger was in excess that I could see Satan's hand in the midst of her. She made offensive comments without any sense.

That day my eyes saw a storm approaching, the winds came from every side, and the thunder was horrendous over our heads. Within me I would ask God to give me words for them. They wanted everyone to tell the story and their version about what had happened that day. From that, they would come to a conclusion and find who was guilty. I felt this was not of God. They began to attack us with their own versions and comments again. They asked me what I had to say about what had transpired. I told the pastor that I came with the objective to reconcile and move forward, not to argue. I shared a scripture from the Bible, and the pastor told me that we are not here to talk about the Bible but to clarify the situation. At that moment I apologized and asked for their forgiveness if I had offended them in anything. I told them I loved them in Christ's love, and I sat down.

When it was my cousin's turn to speak out, she submitted her resignation as president. She felt she should remove herself so there wouldn't be any problems in the manner in which she conducted her presidency. She also read a Bible scripture and told them that her intent was never to offend anyone and asked for forgiveness if she had offended them in anything.

In her position as president, one of her responsibilities was to have vigils, and the majority of the time was dedicated to praying and fasting. Some of the youth were not in accord with this. Their idea of a vigil was for them to have fun and games and not much prayer.

That day we felt that the hymn we were practicing didn't please God. What was happening was not pleasing him. That is why we decided not to participate anymore. Not because we had anything against the youth group. Due to the circumstances, the pastor insisted in finding the guilty ones. My cousin said, "Excuse me, but I wash my hands, I told you what I had to say, I will now leave." She walked toward the door. At that moment, the pastor's wife yelled, if you go beyond that door, forget about your membership with this church. My cousin was surprised; she turned and responded, "Sister, I submit my resignation, but not my church membership." She walked out and closed the door. The pastor then announced through the microphone and said, "Well, brothers, we have just witnessed that sister is no longer a member of this church." My cousin burst out crying, and I couldn't take it anymore. I stood up and told pastor that I wanted to say that what had occurred was not correct. That instant pastor responded, "It's best that you sit down, you already had your turn and have talked too much." I tried to reason with them, but it was in vain. The devil knew well what he wanted to cause that day; he threw a mortal wound. His wife exclaimed in an attacking tone, "Just leave her, can't you see that she is also leaving!" When this happened, I understood that the best thing to do was to leave the meeting. I had already asked for forgiveness, but it wasn't sufficient. I responded, well, I wasn't thinking about leaving, but I believe it is for the best. I walked toward the door and again, the pastor's wife said, "If you go beyond that door forget about your membership with this church." I turned and pointed toward the altar and exclaimed, "Sister, before God, I do not want to leave my membership with this church." Once again, crossing the door, that fatal phrase was heard. "Brothers, we have just witnessed that sister Maria Arias has just left the membership of this church."

I felt as if a sword had pierced my heart, and literally I would have had preferred that instead of those words that someone would have shot me with a gun. I knew for certain where my spirit was going. I still remember the sadness of everyone, especially brother Tapia who was waiting outside. I felt as though I were dying and instantly I thought about the Sunday school children.

Deacons and Officials

After some time I found out that on that day after the meeting, as soon as I left, there was a great silence. The pastor asked the deacons and officials if anyone had anything to say about what had happened, for no one ever spoke or said a word throughout the meeting. At times, it may seem like God did not intuit them to speak, but only he knew what would be and did not allow them to do so. God teaches us that many times he does things like these for our benefit:

> for the benefit of the people standing here,
> that they may believe that you sent me.
>
> John 11:42

It's my understanding that only one sister stood up and said, "I am only going to say one thing. May God have mercy on us for what has happened." They say that the pastor's wife in a broken voice yelled out the pastor's name and said, "Can't you see that they are accusing me?" and began to have an emotional outburst which many stated was her conscious and all-negative spirits and vibes she had that day that caused it. It is my understanding that some church members that were present at the meeting left to another church because of what went on during the meeting. Others, though they did not understand; I thank God they always focused on their love for Jesus and stayed.

My Defeat

For many days I cried and cried and cried with tears of profound pain. I really couldn't find anything that justified what happened. But despite all my pain, I never denied God for that. I didn't feel like going out nor go to church again. My spiritual life was not the same anymore. I realized that I had lost my first love. God knows that I never felt resentment against Pastor and his wife. I was simply very hurt by what had happened. They would tell my mother that they didn't know why I would say that I no longer was a member of the church. On the contrary, they would tell her I was still a member. They never commented to my mother what had happened. Several brothers and sisters from the church would visit me and would give me consoling words. They would ask that I return to the church. Not to pay attention to what had transpired and that God was not at fault and that he still loved me. I knew all this, but the pain I felt was too strong. I asked my God to remove all obstacles between us so that I could serve him as he deserves. Again, my Lord works in mysterious ways, and always has his time.

God Does Not Punish

Shortly after the events mentioned above passed, Pastor's wife was diagnosed with cancer. During those times, many would come to me and say, you see, God is punishing her for her actions. It was hard for me to hear these words. Cancer is a very serious sickness. At that point in my life I had already lost an aunt because of cancer. Another aunt had battled the disease as well, and survived. Despite all things, I would always keep her in my prayers because my aunts would come to my mind, and I would hate to think she was going through cancer. After some time God taught me that he does not punish. However, sin sometimes has serious consequences, and on occasion brings curses into our lives. The verses below are not literal; however, they denote how God feels about losing one of his little ones and warns us that there are consequences for those that dare hurt one of them.

> But if anyone causes one of these little ones who believe in me to sin, it would be better for him to have a large millstone hung around his neck and to be drowned in the depths of the sea. Woe to the world because of the things that cause people to sin! Such things must come, but woe to the man through whom they come!
>
> Matthew 18:6-7

(It is referred to once again in Mark 9:42 and in Luke 17:2.)

> In the same way your Father in heaven is not willing that any of these little ones should be lost.
>
> Matthew 18:14

> A thousand may fall at your side, ten thousand at your right hand; but it will not come near you. You will only observe with your eyes and see the punishment of the wicked.
>
> Psalm 91:7-8

> Wisdom is better than weapons of war, but one sinner destroys much good.
>
> Ecclesiastes 9:18

Not much time passed after this when I was told Pastor's wife had surrendered her sickness into God's hand, and he in his great mercy healed her, and I was happy to know this. I will not say God punished Pastor's wife, because our Holy Father, again, does not punish us; it is we who with our actions, unconsciously, open the door of our hearts for demons to come in and destroy our lives.

> Then it goes and takes with it seven other spirits more wicked than itself, and they go in and live there. And the final condition of that man is worse than the first. That is how it will be with this wicked generation.
>
> Matthew 12:45

Our Holy Father is all about justice, and everybody no matter the age will one day come unto him in Judgment

Day and be judged for what we did and how we lived our lives.

Triumph in the Midst of Defeat

> And we know that in all things God works for the good of those who love him, who have been called according to his purpose.
>
> Romans 8:28

After a short time I could see God's hand as he answered my heart's longing desire. That my parents be revived spiritually, and my sister accepted Jesus as a child. My mother began to go to church, and God began to work with my parents. In time, he gave my parents a beautiful ministry of disseminating Christian music and to preach God's word in the jails of Matamoros, Tamaulipas, Mexico. It was a great victory. Many souls have been touched with his ministry. He has preached and has sent his music to other countries. My parents have various hymns inspired by God, and my father has had the honor of having a CD recording of his ministry. In the middle of all this, God, too, answered my concern of my Sunday school children, for only God knew how much I loved them, and my mother was appointed to be in this place and she did for several years.

Seed That Grew

> I planted the seed, Apollos watered it, but God made it grow.
>
> 1 Corinthians 3:6

As a sophomore in high school, I met a young classmate by the name of Jose. At that time he was involved in gang activity. Back then I would constantly invite him for prayer meetings and speak to him about God's word and his love. I will say this again and again, God has his timing. Sometimes we will not understand why a person did not accept Jesus when you presented the plan of salvation to him or her but that precious seed remains within them. Several years went by. I graduated from high school, went to college, got married, and I was living in Florida with my family. During summer vacation of 2005, I came to Brownsville; my sister had asked me to go pick her up at the university. As I went in to wait for her, I was surprised at what happened. As the elevator doors opened I saw Jose after many years, and the first thing he said was, "Jesus was merciful and saved not only me but my wife when we were in the verge of a divorce, and my family now praises Our Lord Jesus!" I rejoiced for this news. He remembered when he used to laugh and make fun of me whenever I would speak to him about God. Isn't God beautiful, that even in the midst of my pain he gave me several blessings and gifts to rejoice about. Thank you, Lord Jesus!

My Treasure and My Petition

The road may be very long and turbulent when the first love is lost. But after all that had transpired, I always had God present in my life. I always conserved the most precious treasure of having the fear of God and know how to hear his voice. After some time, I was able to talk to the pastor and his wife as if nothing had happened in the past. I achieved total forgiveness when I forgot the past. I never received any apologies nor an explanation for what happened. That was beyond me; my heart was at peace with them. What I couldn't explain is that I couldn't return to the spiritual life I once lived, and my petition was, "God, revive my spirit and resuscitate me, Lord."

The years went by until I learned that God had something special for me. He was still in control of my life, and all that happened was for a purpose. I understood that if God permitted what happened, was because he wanted to use me in a much untraditional way. Therefore, unknowingly, he used me as a light in places in which the majority of people did not know Jesus Christ. Knowing that if I had stayed in that congregation I never would have experienced nor known.

God says in his word:

> Call to me and I will answer you and tell you great and unsearchable things you do not know.
>
> Jeremiah 33:3

In my crossroads I continued working for God; I was always willing to hear his voice. On various occasions I talked to people I didn't know. He always put me in situations and asked that I talk to them about his love.

Vision Given

God showed me a cemetery like no other. It was a cemetery where the souls were dead, buried, and I saw my tomb. At that moment I cried out and exclaimed, "Lord, resuscitate me like Lazarus!" But he soon taught me that it was much more than my burial place and tomb stone. I could see the need but I was there myself dead as the others. Since that day, my cry had been Lord, do with me as you did with Lazarus, again and again. After Sister Dahlia started attending *Misión Divina*, she and I would constantly talk about God's love, miracles, and his doings. I believe God has been making his message clear through preachings and prophecies. I have heard preachings such as: There is a great need for the church to awaken! The church will have a revival! The latter glory will be better than the first! It is time! This year Jesus called my name out of that horrendous tomb and my spirit heard and obeyed as Lazarus did when his name was called.

> After he had said this, he went on to tell them, "Our friend Lazarus has fallen asleep; but I am going there to wake him up."
>
> John 11:11

Jesus referred to death as sleep in the above verse. I believe this verse symbolically teaches us that this is the actual sad state the church is in now. Because of this unfortunate reality, we need to pray, fast, and ask Jesus for a true revival, and that souls are awakened from death. A spiritual cemetery exists and is as real as the air we breathe, and as Jesus told his disciples in the verse stated below.

> ...and for your sake I am glad I was not there, so that you may believe. But let us go to him.
>
> John 11:15

Now allow me to please rephrase and say for your sake I am glad that Jesus was there. He answered my prayer to be resurrected at his will and time. I am glad I can now testify in this book that he has come to me and you may believe that spiritual death is a reality. However, we know there is hope if you have faith and believe in your heart and let God work in your life. He will resurrect, heal and lift you up so that you may fly as an eagle one more time, and he will fulfill his purpose in you and all you have to do is seek and praise him! Amen!

The following scriptures teach us that Jesus did not come to Lazarus immediately; four days had passed; however, Jesus did not worry, for he knew this event was going to be of blessings to many and would transcend the hearts of others for generations to come, me included. Thank you, Lord Jesus.

> After he had said this, he went on to tell them, 'Our friend Lazarus has fallen asleep; but I am going there to wake him up.'
>
> John 11:11

> His disciples replied, 'Lord, if he sleeps, he will get better.' Jesus had been speaking of his death, but his disciples thought he meant natural sleep.
>
> John 11:12-13

So then he told them plainly, 'Lazarus is dead, and for your sake I am glad I was not there, so that you may believe. But let us go to him.'

John 11:14-15

On his arrival, Jesus found that Lazarus had already been in the tomb for four days.

John 11:17

Jesus said to her, 'Your brother will rise again.'

John 11:23

Martha answered, 'I know he will rise again in the resurrection at the last day.'

John 11:24

Jesus said to her, 'I am the resurrection and the life. He who believes in me will live, even though he dies…'

John 11:25

'…And whoever lives and believes in me will never die. Do you believe this?'

John 11:26

Jesus, once more deeply moved, came to the tomb. It was a cave with a stone laid across the entrance. 'Take away the stone,' he said. 'But, Lord,' said Martha, the sister of the dead man, 'by this time there is a bad odor, for he has been there four days.'

John 11:38-39

> Then Jesus said, 'Did I not tell you that if you believed, you would see the glory of God?'
>
> John 11:40

> So they took away the stone. Then Jesus looked up and said, 'Father, I thank you that you have heard me. I knew that you always hear me, but I said this for the benefit of the people standing here, that they may believe that you sent me.'
>
> John 11:41-42

> When he had said this, Jesus called in a loud voice, 'Lazarus, come out!' The dead man came out, his hands and feet wrapped with strips of linen, and a cloth around his face. Jesus said to them, 'Take off the grave clothes and let him go.'
>
> John 11:43-44

I have been working more for God. I have been able to fast and pray and I am beginning to see how once again he is processing me into that spiritual level he wants for not only me but my family to have. I now understand why he also took me from working for the secular world for now and only he knows what will be.

Protect Your Spiritual Life

It is very important that we learn to protect our spiritual life and remember we are God's temple. After my experience I believe I have matured and become more protective of my spiritual life. I have learned to keep my eyes on Jesus only. Every morning I cover myself and my family with the blood of the Holy Lamb and I ask God to send his angels among us. Always décor your spirit with the fruits of the Spirit mentioned in Galatians 5:22-23 and put your spiritual armor of prayer, our sword of the spirit, the shield of faith, and the word of God.

> But the fruit of the Spirit is love, joy, peace, patience, kindness, goodness, faithfulness, gentleness, and self control: against such there is no law.
>
> Galatians 5:22,23

For those that are still sleeping and have been asking God for a revival, be attentive to details and look at your surroundings, for Jesus is calling your name as he did with Lazarus and is saying unto you "Come Out!" To you I say it is time to awaken! Please know that our Lord Jesus knows that you have fallen asleep, but he is going there to wake you up as he did with Lazarus. My God is never late, so you can rest assured your time has come to be awakened and one more time feel his holy spirit flow through your body and bless you with his presence in you. When the time has come, just glorify the Father for taking off your grave clothes and letting you go! I pray and by faith I declare that my testimony serves as a big blessing to many. That those that once were put to sleep or have pain as I had, and for all the church to be awakened leaving only an empty cemetery, letting Jesus remind the angel of death that it is defeated. In Jesus's name, amen!

Juan Arias Bautista and Constanza Mendoza Arias

On March 3, 2010, my father had a stroke that left him weak and unable to walk on his own. Soon after, we learned that there was a big possibility that liquids or food would go to his lungs if he kept eating by his mouth. The doctor recommended that a tube be put through his nose into his stomach in order for him to be fed. After the procedure was done, he was left with the tube for about three days. As a consequence, my dad lost his voice and was left speechless. The first days, my father weakened a whole lot and he would sometimes cry for not being able to express his feelings to us. Within time, the doctor informed us the nose tube could not remain for a prolonged time. He then gave us another alternative, and that was to put a tube in his stomach to be used for feeding until his muscles would gain strength and he could eat on his own. To perform this procedure, a small incision had to be made in his stomach and the tube would pass through there. It was a hard decision to be made being that my dad is diabetic, and this meant he was going to have an open wound until he recuperated. As humans we were sad for my dad, but it was imperative that he would have this procedure performed. Despite this, we knew God had a purpose for what had transpired and this was happening so that he would manifest his glory. At that point we surrendered our father in God's hands and would just pray for him. My father was transferred from the hospital to a rehabilitation center the following week. At the rehab center, he was diagnosed that his throat was paralyzed. Therefore he would permanently not speak nor eat. Against all odds, we praised God in the storm as it kept raining. Shortly, he was also having complications with his blood pressure and sugar levels as he tried to do his walking therapies. This would make all efforts unsuccessful, and my father was not exercising much.

Miracle God Answered

Holy Supper day during evening hours I received a call from my sister in Christ Dahlia. She had just come from Holy Supper celebration at *Misión Divina*. Dahlia shared with me about how my Lord had guided her to purchase a beautiful white material that was to be used as a chair cover during the Holy Supper. The white material was beautiful and really stood out during the service. After the service, Sister Dahlia asked me if she could visit my father at the rehabilitation center. God had spoken to her and instructed her to cover my father from head to toe with the white material and pray for him. Unfortunately it was after visiting hours, and due to hospital rules, the permission to see my father was not granted by the night nurse. The following day during early morning hours Sister Dahlia was obedient and visited him. She anointed him with oil and covered him with the white material as God had directed her to do.

God manifested his glory on my father in a great way. My father said "*Te quiero mucho*" (I love you very much) as his first words and started surprising therapists as he quickly started gaining strength and walking a bit more each day. He was then transferred to a nursing home in order to continue with his therapy sessions. Therapists are amazed of his everyday fast recovery and have in occasions questioned the diagnoses given to him about being permanently paralyzed from his throat. A therapist recently was puzzled, standing next to my father's bed looking at my mom. That day my father was speaking and laughing a bit more; curiously, she asked my mom, do you all pray? My mother answered yes. Then she replied, "That is the only explanation I have, because what my eyes are looking at is a miracle." Quickly after, father started to play with my mom and sister, as he did he would move his arms, legs, and would exercise his voice with laughter.

My mother also had a battle of her own as my dad fought his. Shortly after my father had the stroke, Mom was diagnosed with skin cancer in the early stages. Sister Dahlia felt in her heart that morning to also anoint, pray, and partially cover my mother with the white material. After that day, the doctor was able to remove all damaged skin successfully. He was extremely pleased in the manner in which she quickly recuperated. There was no bruising nor redness as expected for this type of surgery. Thanks to my Lord, he healed my mother. There is no doubt God wanted to protect my mom from such a deadly disease. Sometimes we do not understand God's mysteries but we can only thank him for what he has given us, what he has taken away, and for the new blessings to come.

How Obedience to God with Décor Serves As Blessings for Others

Sister Dahlia shared with me a palm leaf used in *Misión Divina* for Palm Sunday. She explained to me about her pastor's desire to have the temple filled with palm branches and then lead the congregation into the temple. I remembered of Palm Sundays when I used to go to my church. However, I had never heard of or seen anything like this, either. This was refreshing to my soul. I rejoiced to know I was being given a palm that had been blessed by God. Before, during church campaigns I used to receive anointed handkerchiefs or oil, or I was asked to take a picture of a loved one to pray for certain petitions. Sister Dahlia stated, you may share it with friends or family members or just ask God to guide you. That day I had been traveling and our truck was filled with luggage. Our babies had been restless and were having a blast. I turned to see the back seat and I noticed my babies had gotten a hold of the palm leaf, and they were tearing it apart. I immediately spoke to God and asked him, "Father, what am to do with the palm leaf?" He instructed me to give them out to my two sisters-in-law, aunts, family, and Sister Julia to take and share at her mission in Matamoros. I thought to myself as I traveled, *Oh no! I did not keep any for myself and my family*. When we got home, way underneath my luggage I saw a small piece of the palm leaf. God always knows what he is doing. When my little ones played with the leaf, they cut that smaller leaf and left it under the luggage. Those little angels of mine had been used by him. Back in Houston, I placed a palm leaf in my daughter's backpack and left one in my purse. Financially, we have been stable and my daughter's relationship with Jesus is sweet and unique at age five.

On Saturday, May 8, 2010, my husband had to travel down to the valley (which is about a four-hour drive south from where we live) to work on a project down there. My husband works for a cement company as a truck driver. That day they were going to commence the project at 6:00 p.m. Before he left, I gave a palm leaf to my husband and asked him to place it in his wallet, and he did. My husband never asks us to pray for him though we always keep him in our prayers. However, that day he called us before he began on the project and told us, "Pray for me or do what ever you have to do." I was a bit surprised to hear this. After that, my daughter said, "Mom, I'll pray for my dad," and she led the prayer that night. She asked that God send his angels to protect her father. When my husband came back he told me our camera was not working. He said, "I took some pictures, but I am not sure if they came out." I really did not pay much attention that day because I saw the camera and it looked bad. Several days later, my little one year old angel was being a bit curious on top of the bed's headboard. My husband asked that I quickly bring the camera to which I replied, "It is not working; let's see maybe it does take pictures." He took a picture, and all I could see was a broken screen. I took the SD to my laptop to check the pictures there, and then I rejoiced at what I saw. Two of the pictures my husband took that day at work showed a lot of angels around him taking care of them at work. I quickly let my husband know and thanked God for that blessing.

This only goes to prove that God is pleased when his church is open and obedient to his will when it comes to decorations. I believe this is the main motive he inspired this book to us and for all the readers. I will say our Lord is really serious when it comes to décor and obedience. I hope this testimony serves to prove this and I will share these pictures with you for his honor and Glory. Thank you.

Andres G. Muñiz

I was sixty-two years old when I was diagnosed with cancer of the rectum. The year was 1995, the month was June. That same year I had retired in January and was working part time in sales. Through the Veteran's Administration I was sent to San Antonio, Texas, Audie Murphy Hospital for surgery. The surgery was completed and I was sent home for four weeks. I went back to the veteran's hospital and they started chemo and radiation treatments for twenty-eight days. My cancer was in remission for seven years before it appeared again in my liver. For the next three years I went through chemo and radiation, but the cancer would not go away. It did not spread, thank God.

I began to take chemo and radiation in a clinic at McAllen, Texas (which is an hour's drive north of where we live in Brownsville) for thirty days, five days a week, with chemo being injected twenty-four hours per day. I would drive by myself (because my wife was working) everyday of the week to McAllen and back to Brownsville. At the clinic they would give me radiation at 8:30 a.m. and chemo at 9:00 a.m. for two hours every day that I went to the clinic.

At the start of my treatments in the clinic in McAllen, a doctor told my wife I had nine months to live. That's been fifteen years ago, and I am still here with the blessings of my Holy Father. I asked of him to cure and cleanse my body of all cancer, my Holy Father, and he responded. Amen. Also, my Holy Father continues to bless me with the most wonderful and caring wife who has stood by me during these trying times.

In June of 2007, I became very ill due to loss of blood caused by an ulcer and was admitted to a hospital and given two pints of whole blood to offset the loss of blood. All of this time I was asking our Lord for his blessings and that his will be done.

In December 2007, my birthday, I had major surgery on the liver. I was also given radiation to burn the two lesions of the liver. The operation was successful, thank God. I recovered in three months.

However, of the two lesions that were burnt, one of them had a small tumor at the end of the lesion. I had to go through another session of radiation at the cancer center in San Antonio, Texas. I was given five treatments, three one week and two the next week. The Lord blessed me again with his infinite love, and the tumor was burned and did not appear in the following cat scans. I have seen or have been treated by various doctors during the last seven years and they say I should be dead by now; that I have outlived my life. They also say I should not look as healthy as they see me.

I know that all of this was causing a great strain on my wife (bless her heart), but she kept on praying for me, and I for her. When we joined *Misión Divina*, I noticed a change in my wife. There was a transformation in her. There was something peaceful and content in her eyes together with a joyful mood about her. There was also a change in my beliefs about God and his son Jesus Christ. Being a Catholic all my life until I joined *Misión Divina* was quite a change in how we worship God. The change was so great I could not believe how very little was being preached in the Catholic Church compared to *Misión Divina*. I believe that worshipping God in any matter is right, but how we at *Misión Divina* worship God is fulfilling by singing, dancing, and listening to our pastor explain for hours his sermon from the Bible. My church *Misión Divina* is small and very humble now, but with the grace of God, I believe very strongly that the church will flourish and become strong and its parishioners will be many and that the Lord will look kindly and honor his house with many blessings and miracles.

Rosalinda Hernández Zárate

In the name of the Father, the Son, and the Holy Spirit, peace in Jerusalem.

I want to tell you that what I do in the temple decorating is for the glory of my Holy Father and I do it with all my heart, happiness, and joy to please my Heavenly Father.

The enemy (Satan) is always attacking us. He has done it with me physically with back pain, influenza, and other things. I noticed that I would get ill when it was time to decorate the temple for the next month. I did not let him win; I went to the temple feeling ill. I laid at my Holy Father's feet talking to him, praying, and glorifying him. After a few minutes I started feeling a warmth enter me from feet to head, giving me energy and well-being to continue to decorate the temple.

I receive a limited monthly check. Approximately after four months of attending *Iglesia Misión Divina Centrál* in Brownsville, Texas, USA; I started being obedient by giving my tithes, offerings, pacts, and then offerings to the Ornamentation Department. I had faith; I trusted that God would provide for me. He has blessed me; I have food on my table, I make my payments and have enough for my necessities.

Know that God asks of us because he wants to give to us.

So, that is why, show that your trust and faith is in God and our Heavenly Father will make us victorious and if you believe you will see it.

I have faith, I believe and I have seen what God can do.

That's why I ask of you to open your hearts, have faith, believe, and be obedient to our Heavenly Father and you shall have everything.

Our Lord Jesus of Nazareth, the King of kings, is waiting for you; come to him!

Glory to the Almighty God. Amen.

How God Speaks to Me (Rosalinda H. Zárate)

I also want to share with you how God speaks to me. God speaks to people in different ways. If you want to know that when God speaks to you, pray for understanding and how to discern when he speaks to you. Your prayers will not go unanswered. Our Heavenly Father will help you hear him. Just pray, be patient, honor and be obedient to our Heavenly Father, and at the right time you will be blessed because God has a time and order in doing things. That is what happened to me after praying to God to help me discern when he spoke to me.

I realized that my Holy Father speaks to me in visions. My sister and I were shopping for decorations for Christmas 2009. I passed by a display of beautiful glittery filigree gift boxes with a bow on top where it opened. As I saw the red one, a picture came to my mind of Mary, Joseph, and baby Jesus in the gift box. It was as clear as if I had the picture in my hand. On that day, and after what I had experienced on other occasions, it confirmed that my Heavenly Father speaks to me by visions. There is no doubt about it. Amen.

ABOUT THE AUTHORS

Maria de la Luz Arias-Lucio

I was born in Brownsville, Texas. I am happily married and have three wonderful children that pray and love Jesus. My husband is Rumaldo Arriaga Lucio and my children are Sabina del Carmen Lucio, age five, Martha Constanza Lucio, age four, and my one-year-old son Rumaldo Felipe Lucio.

My parents are Juan Arias Bautista and Constanza Mendoza Arias. I was brought up in Brownsville, Texas and am the middle child of a family of two brothers and one sister.

In 1978, Pastor Rita, in collaboration with Martha and Porfirio Mendoza, my grandparents, founded *Templo Aposento Alto* in Matamoros, Tamaulipas, Mexico. The church is still serving and working for God to this day in this city.

I was raised as a Christian, and as a child I was taught by my father to love and fear our God. As a child we would attend *Templo Aposento Alto* and would visit several churches in Brownsville, Texas, USA as well. I accepted Jesus in my heart when I was fifteen years of age; shortly after I was baptized and became an active member of a local Christian church. During the years of my first love, I learned to fast, to pray with authority, to be open to the voice of God, and the importance of having God as the center of our family, and I came to understand that the flesh and the spirit have an ongoing war.

I consider myself a people person; as a young one I always tried to help out by volunteering as a social worker on occasions, engaging in church, school, or community activities or clubs. Also, my career path was always all about helping out, whether I found myself working as a computer specialist, case worker, teacher's assistant, or graphic designer.

I was educated in the Brownsville Independent School District, and I also attended the University of Texas at Brownsville in the studies for a Bachelor of Arts in Applied Science/Computer Information Systems. I have eleven years experience as a Computer Specialist/Graphic Designer and seven years experience in marketing.

I never thought I would be considered an author of this revolutionizing book. Since the day God spoke to my life about this book he inspired me; and in just seconds my Lord revealed to me the objective and chapter titles of this book. I immediately called my sister in Christ Dahlia and began bombarding her with phrases and titles as God did unto me. Probably at that time, Sister Dahlia was puzzled as I first was and wondered what all this was about. Sister Dahlia has known me for several years now. She knew well I am not a writer, nonetheless a person who would come up with such in a matter of seconds to let her know God wanted a book that would educate future generations about how decorations in a temple or church should be chosen. Not to please man, but rather be a pleasant offering to God. Then gradually he opened our spiritual eyes to clearly see and understand his vision. After he taught us he would give us the words to accomplish this publication. Within time, God revealed the majority of this book to Sister Dahlia, and I am honored to have been chosen by God to serve of assistance. I give thanks to God Almighty.

Dahlia Zárate-Muñiz

I was born in Brownsville, Texas, USA. I am married to Andres G. (Andy) Muniz, Jr., originally from Harlingen, Texas.

My parents were Constantino and Lelia Zárate, I am the middle child of three children. I have an older sister and a younger brother.

I was brought up as a Baptist and was baptized on my twelve birthday. I was also baptized in the Jordan River in Israel on November 8, 2008. My great grandfather, Reverend Toribio G. Hernández, was the founder of the First Mexican Baptist Church in Brownsville, Texas, USA. The church officially opened its doors on October 14, 1909 and celebrated its one hundredth anniversary on October 14, 2009.

I was educated in the Brownsville Independent School District. I received an Associate in Applied Science Degree from Texas Southmost College and received my Bachelors of Science Degree from the University of Texas Pan American.

I was also a licensed cosmetologist for the State of Texas from 1979 thru 2007.

Honored

My husband served on the Brownsville Housing Authority for ten years. However, he served as chairman for seven consecutive years. A housing development of ninety-two lots was approved by the authority on twenty acres of land. The housing commissioners wanted to honor their wives by naming a street after each one of them. Consequently, a street was named after me, "Dahlia Circle." This is a huge blessing and great honor my Holy Father bestowed on me.

Another honor my Holy Father allowed was the acceptance of my recommendation to name a brand new housing complex, "Tropical Gardens at Boca Chica."

My Holy Father also honored our marriage. We were recognized as a *"Matrimonio Magnifico"* (Magnificent Marriage) in Cameron County, Texas, USA in 2008.

Community Contributions

I served on the University of Texas Brownsville Dyslexia Committee in planning and coordinating a Dyslexia Conference for the community serving three counties in South Texas, USA.

I chaired the committee on Discharge Policy Procedures for the Homeless Network of the Rio Grande Valley. I planned, coordinated and implemented a workshop between federal, state and local law enforcement agencies and our county homeless providers. I also participated in the development of a regional plan to end chronic homelessness.

I served on the committee in the planning, coordinating, and implementation of the 2006 Congressional Veterans Summit in Cameron County, Texas, USA, and again in 2009.

Employment Experience

As part of my responsibilities for my previous employer, I established linkages throughout the community, as well as served as a liaison with federal, state, local agencies and regional groups in matters concerning the coordination of plans and services.

I also conducted a training with the Texas Workforce Commission for the Southern region of Texas. I coordinated and helped implement the transition from State to local Workforce Board control. I planned, designed, organized and conducted educational and training programs, analyzed training needs, developed and prepared training materials, and coordinated and conducted training sessions.

My duties and responsibilities also entailed that I plan, assign, and supervise the work of others. I managed and evaluated a broad range of workforce development program contracts and ensured contract deliverables and performance measures were met as well as wrote concise reports.

I was also an instructor with the Brownsville Independent School District for the Adult Continuing

Education Department. I taught the basic subjects required for a person to obtain their G.E.D. as well as assisted students in achieving employment techniques and identifying sources of information about available jobs.

Bless Israel and You Will Be Blessed

My husband and I are members of the Temple Institute in Jerusalem and partners with the International Fellowship of Christians and Jews.

> Pray for the peace of Jerusalem: they shall prosper that love thee.
>
> Psalm 122:6 (KJV)

> I will bless those who bless you...
>
> Genesis 12:3

Ornamentation Director Iglesia Misión Divina Central

In June of 2007, my Holy Father led me to *Iglesia Misión Divina Centrál* in Brownsville, Texas, USA. My Holy Father called me for his ministry in 2008. I officially became a member of *Misión Divina* in the summer of 2009. We carry the divine mission of taking the revival message to the world with signs and wonders. To date, there are approximately eighteen *Misiónes Divina* throughout Mexico, the United States, Guatemala, Canada, and Dominican Island. We also have a radio program *Radio Vida* 1290AM in Weslaco, Texas, USA, which reaches USA, Mexico, Argentina, Venezuela, Peru, and Honduras. A television program as well, *Genesis TV* channel 50, Matamoros, Tamaulipas, Mexico.

As per my Holy Father's will, I officially became the Ornamentation Director for *Iglesia Misión Divina* on March 8, 2009. I feel honored and humbled that my Holy Father chose me to decorate his house of worship. It truly is a great honor. As I reflect, I recall standing on the shore of the Great Sea my first evening in Israel. Looking at that massive body of water, with the light of the beautiful full moon reflecting on the peaceful water, I feel like one of those grains of sand, that from a multitude of people he chose me.

Throughout 2009 I also accompanied Mark Edward Meinschein, missionary evangelist from Rays of Hope Ministries in Dallas, Texas, USA to a hospital in Matamoros, Tamaulipas, Mexico. We would pray for the sick and dying patients, both young and old. He would bless the patients with prayers, comfort, stuffed animals, toiletries, and medical supplies.

MISION DIVINA'S ORNAMENTATION DEPARTMENT LOGO

Through God's inspiration the logo for the Ornamentation Department was created. The logo consists of a shield and a sword.

> ... And a flaming sword flashing back and forth.
>
> Genesis 3:24

The shield and sword represent the armor of God. The logo also symbolizes that *Iglesia Misión Divina Central* is a warrior Church.

> For we wrestle not against flesh and blood, but against principalities, against powers, against the rulers of the darkness of this world, against spiritual wickedness in high places.
>
> Ephesians 6:12 (KJV)

The weapons we fight with are not the weapons of the world. On the contrary, they have divine power to demolish strongholds.

2 Corinthians 10:4

He is your shield and helper and your glorious sword.

Deuteronomy 33:29

…By the armor of righteousness on the right hand and on the left.

2 Corinthians 6:7 (KJV)

Shield

Above all, taking the shield of faith, wherewith ye shall be able to quench all the fiery darts of the wicked.

Ephesians 6:16 (KJV)

My God……my shield…

2 Samuel 22:3

He is a shield for all who take refuge in him.

2 Samuel 22:31

He is my shield…

Psalm 18:2

You give me your shield of victory.

Psalm 18:35

But you are a shield around me, O Lord.

> Psalm 3:3

My shield is God Most High…

> Psalm 7:10

He is our help and our shield.

> Psalm 33:20

His faithfulness will be your shield…

> Psalm 91:4

Sword

…And the sword of the Spirit, which is the word of God.

> Ephesians 6:17

…And a flaming sword flashing back and forth to guard the way to the tree of life.

> Genesis 3:24

For the word of God is living and active. Sharper than any double-edged sword it penetrates to even dividing soul and spirit…

> Hebrews 4:12

If he does not relent he will sharpen his sword…

> Psalm 7:12

> Out of his mouth comes a sharp sword with which to strike down the nations.
>
> Revelation 19:15

> …And out of his mouth came a sharp double-edged sword.
>
> Revelations 1:16

Logo Colors

White

Holiness of God:

> …And his clothes became as white as the light.
>
> Matthew 17:2

> …And his clothes were white as snow.
>
> Matthew 28:3

> His clothing was as white as snow.
>
> Daniel 7:9

Victory:

> They will walk with me, dressed in white, for they are worthy.
>
> Revelation 3:4

Faithful, True:

> I saw heaven standing open and there before me was a white Horse, whose rider is called Faithful and True.
>
> Revelation 19:11

Purple

Royalty, Kingship:

> ...And the purple garments worn by the kings...
>
> Judges 8:26

Blue

Holy Spirit, Sky and God above Us, Heaven, Divinity, God's Glory:

> Above the expanse over their heads was what looked like a throne of sapphire and high above on the throne was a figure like that of a man.
>
> Ezekiel 1:26

Royalty:

> Make the Tabernacle with ten curtains of finely twisted linen and blue...
>
> Exodus 26:1

Israel (stripe on tallit):

> ...You are to make tassels on the corners of your garments, with a blue cord on each tassel.
>
> Numbers 15: 38

The Art of Decoration

SYMBOLISM COLORS

Red:

Blood of Jesus Christ:

> But with the precious blood of Christ.
>
> 1 Peter 1:19

Blood:

> The water looked red—like blood.
>
> 2 Kings 3:22

Cleansing:

> And the blood of Jesus, his son, purifies us from all sin.
>
> 1 John 1:7

Sins:

> Though your sins are like scarlet...
>
> Isaiah 1:18

White:

Holiness of God:

> And his clothes became as white as the light.
>
> Matthew 17:2

> And his clothes were white as snow.
>
> Matthew 28:3

> His clothing was as white as snow.
>
> Daniel 7:9

Victory:

> They will walk with me, dressed in white, for they are worthy.
>
> Revelation 3:4

Faithful, True:

> I saw heaven standing open and there before me was a white Horse, whose rider is called Faithful and True.
>
> Revelation 19:11

Purple:

Royalty, Kingship:

> And the purple garments worn by the kings…
>
> Judges 8:26

Blue:

Holy Spirit, Sky, and God Above Us; Heaven, Divinity, God's Glory:

> Above the expanse over their heads was what looked like a throne of sapphire and high above on the throne was a figure like that of a man.
>
> Ezekiel 1:26

Royalty:

> Make the Tabernacle with ten curtains of finely twisted linen and blue…
>
> Exodus 26:1

Gold:

Royalty:

> They were dressed in white and had crowns of gold on their heads.
>
> Revelation 4:4

> And placed a crown of pure gold on his head.
>
> Psalm 21:3

Silver:

Purity, Truth:

> And the words of the Lord are flawless, like silver refined in a furnace of clay purified seven times.
>
> Psalm 12:6

Ivory:

Royalty, Beauty, Glory, Holiness:

> Then the king made a great throne inlaid with ivory.
>
> 1 Kings 10:18

> God is seated on his holy throne.
>
> Psalm 47:8

Green:

Growth:

> They are like plants in the field, like tender green shoots like grass sprouting on the roof.
>
> 2 Kings 19:26

Fruitful:

> I am like a green pine tree, your fruitfulness comes from me.
>
> Hosea 14:8

Yellow:

Light, Glory:

> For the Glory of God gives it light.
>
> Revelation 21:23

> His face shone like the sun and his clothes became as white as the light.
>
> Matthew 17:2

Sunshine, Brightness of Christ:

> His face was like the sun shining in all its brilliance.
>
> Revelation 1:16

God's Fire:

> Then the Lord rained down burning sulfur.
>
> Genesis 19:24

Black:

Death:

> At twilight, as the day was fading as the dark of night set in.
>
> Proverbs 7:9

> My skin grows black and peels.
>
> Job 30:30

Famine, bloodshed:

> And there before me was a black horse.
>
> Revelation 6:5

SYMBOLISM NUMBERS

1—God:

> In the beginning God created the heavens and the earth.
>
> Genesis 1:1 (KJV)

> In that day shall there be one Lord, and his name one.
>
> Zechariah 14:9

2—Unity:

> Two are better than one.
>
> Ecclesiastes 4:9 (KJV)

3—Holy Trinity; Divine Perfection:

> And I will pray the Father, and he shall give you another Comforter, that he may abide with you forever.
>
> John 14:16 (KJV)

> And ye shall receive the gift of the Holy Ghost.
>
> Acts 2:38 (KJV)

4—All That Is Created: (i.e., North, South, East, West; Spring, Summer, Autumn, Winter; length, width, height, time)

> In the beginning GOD created the heaven and the earth.
>
> Genesis 1:1 (KJV)

5—Grace:

> For by grace are ye saved through faith; and that not of yourselves: it is the gift of God.
>
> Ephesians 2:8 (KJV)

6—Number of Man: Man was created on the sixth day.

> And God said, Let us make man in our image, after our likeness.
>
> Genesis 1:26 (KJV)

7—Completion; God's Seal of Approval:

> And on the seventh day God ended his work which he had made.
>
> Genesis 2:2 (KJV)

> And God blessed the seventh day, and sanctified it.
>
> Genesis 2:3 (KJV)

8 – New Beginnings: From Noah's Ark, eight souls were saved after the flood.

> Wherein few, that is eight souls were saved by water.
>
> 1 Peter 3:20 (KJV)

9—Judgment: This can either be judgment of life, such as the gifts of the Spirit (e.g., the word of wisdom, word of knowledge, faith, healing, working of miracles, prophecy, discerning of spirits, diverse kind of tongue, interpretation of tongues).

> But the manifestation of the Spirit is given to every man to profit Withal …
>
> 1 Corinthians 12: 7-11 (KJV)

Or Judgment of death; nine people are stoned in the Bible. Leviticus 24:10-11; Numbers 15:32-36, Acts 7:54-60, Joshua 7: 25; I Kings 12:18; 2 Chronicles 24:21; Acts 14:19-20; I Kings 21:9; Judges 9:53.

10 -Perfection of Divine Order: Ten Commandments, Exodus 20:3-17; Ten Righteous, Genesis 18:32, "What if only ten can be found there?"

11- Disorder:

> See if you can lure him into showing you the secrets of his great strength and how we can overpower him so we may tie him up and

subdue him. Each one of us will give you eleven hundred shekels of silver.

Judges 16:5

The eleven hundred shekels of silver that were taken from you and about which I heard you utter a curse.

Judges 17:2-4

12 - City of GOD; Governmental Perfection:

And showed me the Holy City, Jerusalem, coming down out of heaven from God.

Revelation 21: 10-21

Twelve Apostles,

He appointed twelve—designating them apostles...

Mark 3:14

CLOSING

> Just as Moses lifted up the snake in the desert, so the Son of Man must be lifted up…
>
> John 3:14

Our sole purpose of writing this book is to please God and do his will. For if we do not speak, the rocks will; or we believe we should rephrase and say, we used to be rocks that are now speaking because of his grace and glory. We have chosen to listen and be obedient to our Lord and Savior. The intent of this book is not to offend anyone, but to teach and enlighten the reader about what our Lord wants and expects from us in order for him to bless us. We pray that this book brings an understanding and many blessings to your life and your church. Know that nothing is in vain when we are on the Lord's path.

> He who has an ear, let him hear what the Spirit says to the churches.
>
> Revelation 2:7

To God be all praise and honor!
Amen!

CHURCH NAME AND ADDRESS

Iglesia Misión Divina Centrál
www.misiondivina.com
2105 E. Fourteenth Street
Brownsville, Texas, USA 78520

CONTACT THE AUTHORS

You can follow the authors on facebook.
Maria Arias-Lucio
Dahlia Zárate-Muñiz

Author photography & lighting by: Rosalinda H. Zárate
Lighting Assistant: Sylvia Vera
*Please include your testimony or help received
from this book when you write.*

RESOURCES

All Bible scriptures are from the (NIV) *New International Version Study Bible* unless noted (KJV) *King James Version*
Dake's Annotated Reference Bible
Numbers that Preach by Troy Brewer
Mysteries of the Glory Unveiled by David Herzog
Matthew Henry's Commentary on the Whole Bible
Jewish Encyclopedia

The Perfect Work: Poems of Hafiz
Live at Lipinsky Hall: *Thomas Rain Crowe & The Boatrockers*

MEMOIR

Zoro's Field: My Life in the Appalachian Woods

ESSAYS

The End of Eden

AUTOBIOGRAPHICAL FICTION

A House of Girls